New Perspectives

Politics, Religion and Conflict in Mid-Antrim
1911-1914

Philip Orr

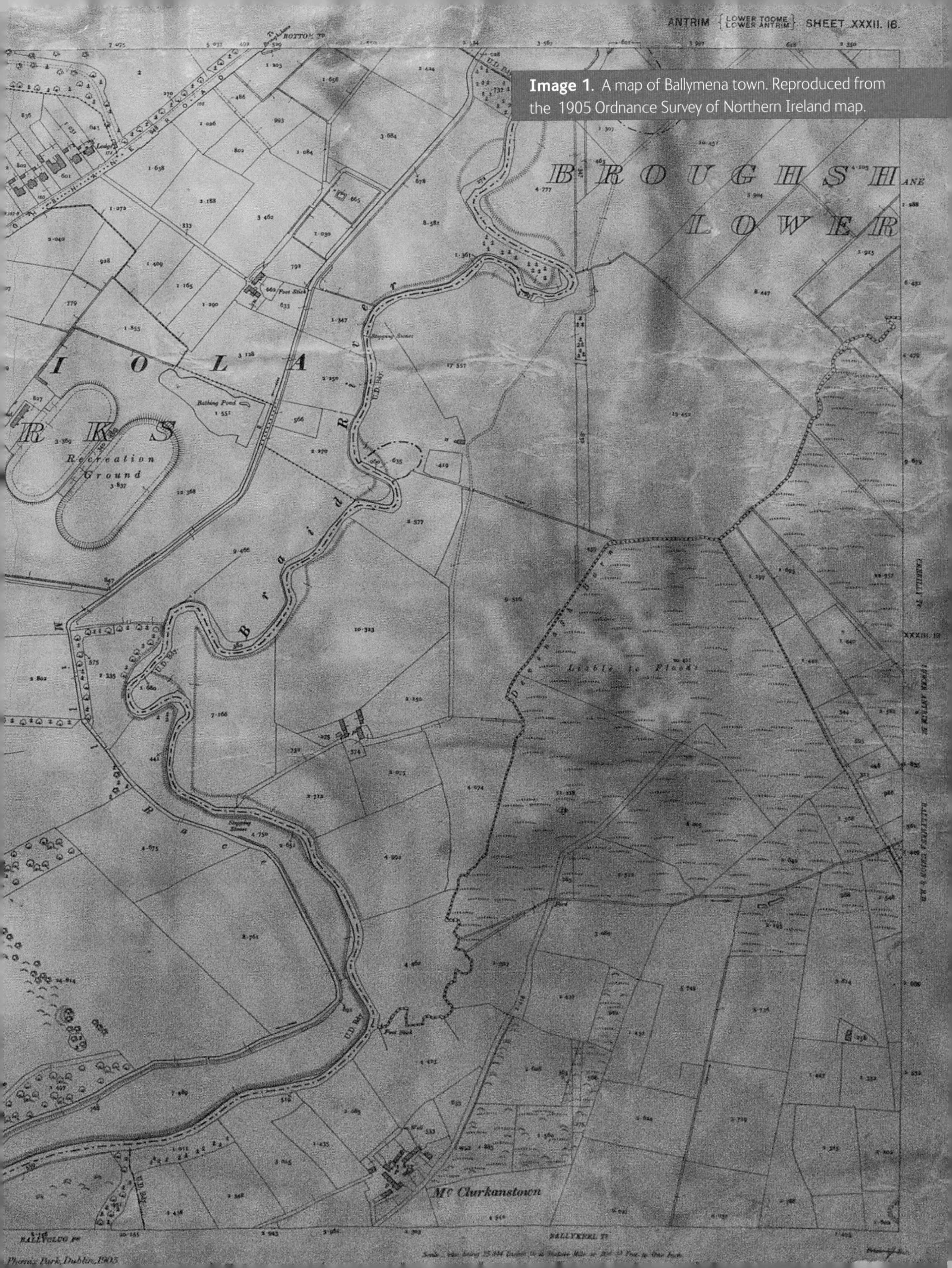

Image 1. A map of Ballymena town. Reproduced from the 1905 Ordnance Survey of Northern Ireland map.

New Perspectives - Politics, Religion and Conflict in Mid-Antrim 1911-1914

-

Philip Orr

-

Published by Mid-Antrim Museum, 2011

ISBN: 978-0-9568586-0-3

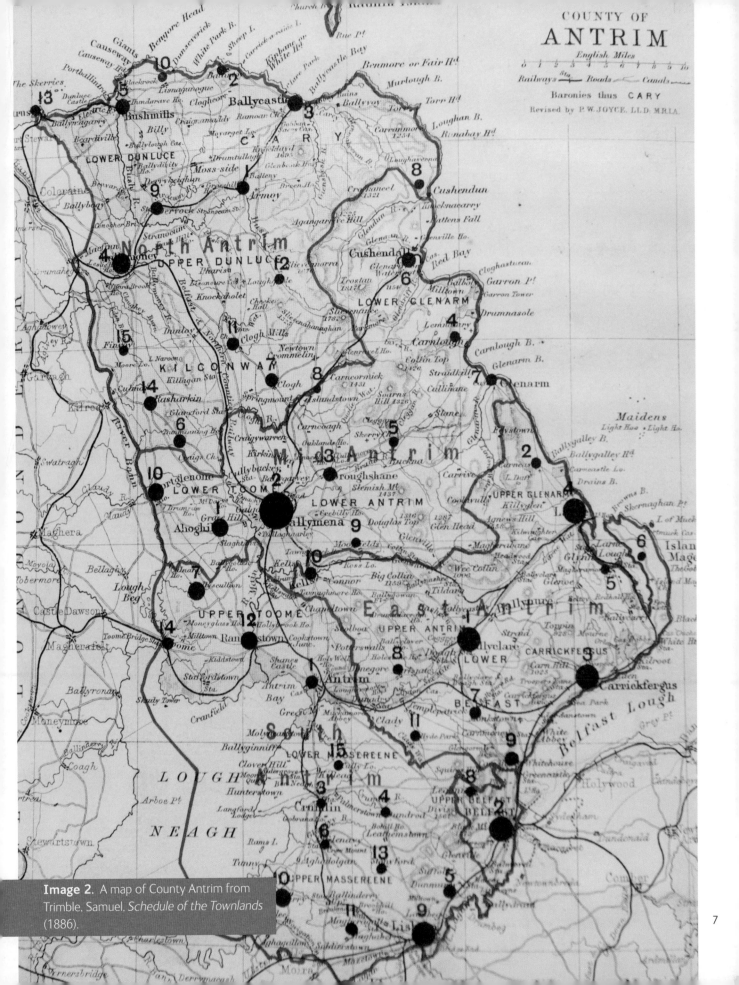

Image 2. A map of County Antrim from Trimble, Samuel, *Schedule of the Townlands* (1886).

Contents

List of Images   10

Foreword   13

Preface   17

Introduction: The Brink of War
The last Bank Holiday weekend of peacetime   19

Ulster politics before the outbreak of the Great War   21

Outbreak of war   22

Chapter One: Mid-Antrim on the Eve of Change
The Mid-Antrim gentry   25

The 'working class'   28

Farmers, merchants and rising prosperity   31

Unionist culture and devotion to the Empire   33

Protestant and Catholic cultures in Mid-Antrim   36

The growth of civic life in Ballymena   38

Ballymena in an era of growing industrial unrest   42

Local women in the era of the suffragettes   44

The growth of nationalist self-confidence in Mid-Antrim   45

From 18th century republicans to opponents of Home Rule   48

First unionist reactions to the 3rd Home Rule Bill in Mid-Antrim   50

Local unionist rhetoric and the beginning of organised resistance   52

Chapter Two: 1912 - The Year of the Covenant
The local growth of Presbyterian unionism   57

The dilemma for Liberal Party supporters in Ballymena   60

The development of a local unionist leadership   61

Religious animosity and street politics in Ballymena   62

Political combat in the local press   68

Mid-Antrim politics during the spring and summer of 1912.   69

The 'Castledawson Sunday School outrage' and its aftermath   72

Signing the Ulster Covenant in Ballymena   76

The religious composition of Ballymena and district in the era of the Covenant   80

The beginnings of a loyalist army   81

Christmas 1912   82

Contents

Chapter Three: 1913 - The Year of the Volunteers

The Ulster Volunteer Force is officially formed 85

Opposition to the unionist project 87

Training the local Ulster Volunteer Force 88

Edward Carson and James Craig visit Ballymena - July 1913 89

The composition of Buckna rural U.V.F. unit 95

The 1st Battalion of the U.V.F. North Antrim Regiment begins to take shape 97

The beginnings of the Irish National Volunteers 99

Caution, scepticism and opposition - some Protestant reactions to militarised unionism 99

A liberal critique of Ballymena's unionist leaders 102

Training and the rhetoric intensify within Ballymena's unionist community 104

Chapter Four: 1914 - The Year of the Guns

Motorcars, cavalry, rations and signals - expanding the capacity of the Mid-Antrim U.V.F. 111

The threat of British military suppression of the U.V.F. - March 1914 112

Medicine, uniforms and plans for war 114

Relationships between police, unionists and nationalists in the spring of 1914 115

A camp of instruction for the local Ulster Volunteers 116

Five hundred and fifty German guns for Mid-Antrim unionists - April 1914 117

Mid-Antrim prepares for battle - April and May 1914 119

The Home Rule Bill passes 122

The growth of the National Volunteers and the lurch towards civil war 123

Ballymena unionists face the doomsday scenario - June and July 1914 128

The last few days of peacetime 131

Conclusion: August 1914 and Beyond
Mid-Antrim and the Great War 137

The Easter Rising and its aftermath 140

New perspectives 142

Bibliography 146

Acknowledgements 149

List of Images

Image 1. A map of Ballymena town. Reproduced from the 1905 Ordnance Survey of Northern Ireland Map. (Mid-Antrim Museum collection)

Image 2. A map of County Antrim from Trimble, Samuel, *Schedule of the Townlands* (1886). (Mid-Antrim Museum collection)

Image 3. An array of documents from the Mid-Antrim Museum U.V.F archive.

Image 4. The Braid Water Mill. (Mid-Antrim Museum collection)

Image 5. Crebilly Castle. (Mid-Antrim Museum collection)

Image 6. Rock View, Ballymena. (Mid-Antrim Museum collection)

Image 7. Lancashire's chemist shop delivering mineral water. (Mid-Antrim Museum collection)

Image 8. Empire Day in Galgorm village. (Young Collection, Mid-Antrim Museum)

Image 9. The proclamation of the accession of George V in Ballymena. (Young collection, Mid-Antrim Museum)

Image 10. The Congregational Church in Kinhilt Street, Ballymena. (Mid-Antrim Museum collection)

Image 11. Galgorm Road, Ballymena. (Mid-Antrim Museum collection)

Image 12. Mill Street, Ballymena. (Mid-Antrim Museum collection)

Image 13. The Cottage Hospital, Ballymena. (Mid-Antrim Museum collection)

Image 14. Sir Arthur O'Neill. (Mid-Antrim Museum collection)

Image 15. Taise Banner. (Ballycastle Museum collection)

Image 16. Proclaiming the accession of King George V at the Old Town Hall in Ballymena. (Young collection, Mid-Antrim Museum)

Image 17. Ballymena Castle. (Mid-Antrim Museum collection)

Image 18. Anti-Home Rule postcard. (Mid-Antrim Museum collection)

Image 19. Pro-Home Rule postcard. (Item on display at the Mid-Antrim Museum - on loan from the Linenhall Library)

Image 20. Lower Bridge Street, Ballymena. (Mid-Antrim Museum collection)

Image 21. Church Street, Ballymena. (Mid-Antrim Museum collection)

Image 22. Garfield Place, Ballymena. (Mid-Antrim Museum collection)

Image 23. John Patrick McCann. (Image donated by the McCann family)

Image 24. Boy Scouts with their scoutmaster, outside Galgorm National School. (Young collection, Mid-Antrim Museum)

List of Images

Image 25. St. Patrick's Church of Ireland in Castle Street. (Mid-Antrim Museum collection)

Image 26. The People's Park, Ballymena. (Mid-Antrim Museum collection)

Image 27. The Pentagon, Ballymena. (Mid-Antrim Museum collection)

Image 28. A parade along the Galgorm Road. (Mid-Antrim Museum collection)

Image 29. Local U.V.F. men practising drill in the courtyard of Galgorm Castle. (Young collection, Mid-Antrim Museum)

Image 30. A livestock mart on the Fair Hill, Ballymena. (Mid-Antrim Museum collection)

Image 31. Lapel badge created for Sir Edward Carson's visit to Mid-Antrim in July 1913. (John Pattison collection)

Image 32. A page from an album belonging to the Young family. (Young collection, Mid-Antrim Museum)

Image 33. Craig and Carson's visit to Galgorm Castle. (Young collection, Mid-Antrim Museum)

Image 34. A souvenir bust of Sir Edward Carson with a Ballymena crest. (Mid-Antrim Museum collection)

Image 35. The armband of an Ulster Volunteer in the 1st Battalion, North Antrim Regiment of the U.V.F. (John Pattison collection)

Image 36. The former facade of Wellington Street Presbyterian Church, Ballymena. (Mid-Antrim Museum collection)

Image 37. A slouch hat belonging to the Irish Citizens' Army. (Item on display in Mid-Antrim Museum - on loan from the National Museum of Ireland)

Image 38. A replica tunic belonging to the Irish Citizens' Army. (Item on display in Mid-Antrim Museum - on loan from the National Museum of Ireland)

Image 39. A crowd gathers in the Protestant Hall on the Galgorm Road, Ballymena to hear anti-Home Rule speeches. (Image courtesy of *Ballymena Observer*)

Image 40. A prayer card belonging to an Ulster Volunteer. (John Pattison collection)

Image 41. Ulster Volunteers from a Ballymena family. (John Pattison collection)

Image 42. Ulster Volunteer William Ross, with his two sisters, both U.V.F. nurses. (Mid-Antrim Museum collection)

Image 43. An R.I.C. badge. (Item housed at Mid-Antrim Museum, on loan from James McNeill)

Image 44. A motor corps badge of the Ulster Volunteers. (On loan from Alan Stewart to the John Pattison collection)

List of Images

Image 45. A U.V.F. bayonet and scabbard. (John Pattison collection)

Image 46. Frederick d'Arcy, Bishop of Down, Dromore and Connor, blesses the colours of the 1st Battalion of the North Antrim Regiment (Young collection, Mid-Antrim collection)

Image 47. The U.V.F. stamp was placed on each rifle butt and the guns were registered. (John Pattison collection)

Image 48. A bugle belonging to the Irish Citizens' Army. (Item on display in Mid-Antrim Museum - on loan from the National Museum of Ireland)

Image 49. Captain Jack White from Broughshane on parade with the Irish Citizens' Army. (Mid-Antrim Museum collection)

Image 50. An Ulster Volunteer knapsack. (John Pattison collection)

Image 51. A U.V.F. bandolier, for carrying bullets. (John Pattison collection)

Image 52. Craigywarren Ulster Volunteers. (Mid-Antrim Museum collection)

Image 53. A Mauser Rifle. (John Pattison collection)

Image 54. Harryville U.V.F. roll of honour. (Mid-Antrim Museum)

Foreword

Museums have an important role to play in addressing issues surrounding cultural and personal identities. By creating a public space, they provide a platform for exploring and understanding our own histories.

Mid-Antrim Museum has striven over the years to reveal the local stories which are played out against a backdrop of wider national and international events.

The museum's unique collection of documents relating to the local Ulster Volunteer Force has allowed for an extensive exploration of the turbulent period leading up to the outbreak of World War I, as it played out in the provincial market town of Ballymena and its hinterland.

This publication aims to encourage constructive investigation and debate on a critical moment in Ulster's history, one that represents a milestone in the road to the creation of the Northern Ireland state. *New Perspectives* presents new, unpublished source material which, in conjunction with other contemporary sources, offers fresh insights into the local experience of the 1911-1914 period.

Collaboration with Philip Orr has helped the museum and its collection to make tangible connections with our past. It is hoped that this present study can encourage mutual understanding of our history and cultural heritage.

Shirin Murphy
Acting Curator
Mid-Antrim Museums Service

O. Form C. 2.

ULSTER VOLUNTEE

County _____ 1st Batt. N.

Division _____ Ahoghill

District _____

Locality _____ Ballymena

NAME (Surname first
Christian Name afterwards)

LEADER.

McAuley Joseph   A   Alfred Str

Herbert Jos Joseph   A   2 Francis

Seemons William   A   3 Salisbu

                                 A

through Mr. Geo. Young.

O. Form C. 2.

UNTEER

FORCE.

trim Reg.

which enlisted in
Ulster Division the
Sept 26th 1914

*ORGANIZATION
NUMBER.

mid.

a & Carclin

Date

ADDRESS

DRESS.

Place Ballymena A 14348
t.   9
og.   50
                          1
                          2

Cul

ory Gla

Cul

Road

Preface

New Perspectives originated with the discovery of a collection of documents pertaining to the years 1913-14, which had belonged to headquarters staff of the local Ulster Volunteer Force (U.V.F.) and which is now in the possession of the Museum. The collection includes correspondence and muster rolls. In order to analyse this material within its organisational contexts, other relevant U.V.F. archives in the Public Record Office of Northern Ireland had to be explored. The Irish Census for 1911 also proved to be an invaluable aid in determining the social composition of the anti-Home Rule movement in the area. Local newspaper reports from the period provided a very fruitful source, as a detailed story of unionism in Mid-Antrim from 1911 to the foundation of the U.V.F. in January 1913 began to emerge, with its array of political rallies, legal disputes, fiery sermons and day-to-day evidence of the rapid move towards militarisation of the pro-Union project.

However, it became clear from these newspapers and from diaries, autobiographies and local accounts of the period that the unionist story was interwoven with the story of nationalism and with other important trends such as the rise of militant labour politics and the emergence of the movement for female emancipation. The rich everyday civic life of Mid-Antrim, as described in such sources, also needed inclusion in order to provide an appropriate social background to stirring political developments. However, the archival sources for local nationalism, suffragette politics and labour relations are much less rich than the sources for unionism and so the story of the anti-Home Rule project in Mid-Antrim does tend to dominate this account of the highly politicised pre-war years in Ballymena and its hinterland.

The author of this book is aware that he has given a great deal of prominence to political and religious rhetoric which was designed to stir up local sentiment, rather than looking at the more carefully articulated economic theory and cultural argumentation which took place within the high politics of this era, in places far removed from the public parks, laneways, parochial halls and meeting-houses of County Antrim. However, it is the contention of the author that the production and reception of local rhetoric by clergy and other civic figures has often been overlooked in past accounts of this period of Ulster history - and that this oversight needs to be addressed.

It should be stressed that while this book sets out to look at various kinds of political and social conflict in Mid-Antrim in the years leading up to the Great War, the author has looked at local religion mainly as it interacts with these disputes. Church life in the district did of course go on in many other quiet and affirmative ways that did not connect with the political conflict. However, that ongoing saga of daily faith does not figure in this particular account, which seeks to illuminate the often contentious role of religion in Ulster politics during the Home Rule Crisis.

It must also be noted that in the period 1911-14, the words unionism and loyalism were fairly interchangeable. They are not synonymous today, within a society where many people see themselves as adherents of unionism but would reject the assertion that they are loyalists. When these two terms are used in *New Perspectives*, the reader should assume that they cover much the same descriptive ground, with loyalism perhaps referring rather more to cultural phenomena and unionism to the political practice that accompanied that culture.

The precise bounds of the geographical term 'Mid-Antrim' are of course open to interpretation. For the purposes of this account, the author has not aligned 'Mid-Antrim' along the boundaries of the political constituency of that name which existed until 1922, although there is an overlap. Rather it seemed best to consider the area which the local battalion of the Ulster Volunteer Force considered to be both its zone of influence and its catchment area. This was very much centred on Ballymena but extended westwards towards the River Bann and also eastwards towards the Antrim Glens, even though districts such as the Glens did constitute a distinct geo-political space. Throughout this account, Mid-Antrim may also be thought of as an area extending almost ten miles south from Ballymena (though not as far as either Antrim town or Randalstown) and up to fifteen miles northwards from the town.

However, this account also draws on material relating to other parts of Ulster - mainly adjacent ones - particularly when trying to understand the nationalism with which local unionists were at odds. This authorial decision was due to the paucity of material on militant nationalism in and around Ballymena during the Home Rule Crisis.

Introduction

The last Bank Holiday weekend of peacetime

On Tuesday, 4th August 1914, Ballymena went back to work after the Bank Holiday weekend, like most other towns in the British Isles. The weather for the early part of the holiday had been warm and reasonably sunny. Many of those who could afford to do so had left the County Antrim town for the seaside. Some adventurous holidaymakers on that August Monday had enjoyed a boat-trip on the Irish Sea, prompted by recent advertisements in the Ballymena papers which described in glowing terms a pleasure cruise on board the new turbine steamer, the *Princess Victoria*, which took passengers north from Larne along the Antrim coast, then around the rocky cliffs of Rathlin Island before returning home.

During the four-hour cruise there was ample opportunity for the voyagers to sample 'luncheons and teas' in the ship's cafe as they watched the scenery go by. It was a pleasure which was spoilt somewhat on the way back to the harbour due to mist and rain.

For those who could only dream of such luxuries, there was the possibility of some cheaper forms of entertainment. On Tuesday 4th August, the main feature in Ballymena's cinema was a silent movie called *Black Spot*, about a Russian professor with revolutionary opinions who is exiled in England and leads a plot to assassinate the heir to the Romanoff throne, who is visiting London. The dastardly plot is thwarted by the timely intervention of the local police. Other short films in the program included *The Circumstantial Nurse* and *Biddy on her Mettle*.

By early on Tuesday morning, it was life as usual in Ballymena. Shops did brisk business, as was invariably the case in this busy market town. Local mills and factories operated their daily shifts. The Ballymena Urban District Council held its monthly meeting and considered a wide range of issues, from the salaries of the town's sanitary officers to the re-painting of seats in the town's cemetery. One councillor described problems caused by somebody dumping rubbish in the small lake in the People's Park. Another councillor noted the flooding which had taken place on the Cullybackey Road during a recent deluge. The council decided to write off the debt incurred by one local businessman on the Doury Road who had experienced a fire on his premises and was struggling to repay the cost incurred by calling out the Ballymena firemen with their 'steam engine' and horses. The councillors also considered whether a lamp in High Street should be moved to Boyd's Entry in order to help the workers who made their way in and out of 'Mr Clarke's boot factory' in darkness, throughout the long winter months.

But this modest picture of civic order at the end of a bright holiday weekend hides the reality that Ballymena - like almost every other town in the north of Ireland - was deep in the grip of political turmoil. On Monday, two hundred men, dressed in a smart, improvised military uniform and carrying rifles, had assembled at Ballymena railway station and boarded their specially chartered train for the northern seaside town of Ballycastle.

This was a unit from the 1st North Antrim Battalion of the Ulster Volunteer Force (U.V.F.), a citizens' army which had been formed a year and a half before to resist the British Government's plans for a new 'Home Rule' parliament in Ireland. Ballymena and much of the Mid-Antrim countryside which surrounded it was a heartland of Ulster Protestant political culture which dreaded being ruled from Dublin, seeing this as a recipe for impoverishment, diminution of British citizenship and domination by the Irish Catholic Church.[1]

Most local Protestants thought of themselves collectively as 'unionists' and 'loyalists', dedicated to a deep unity with Britain, even though Ulster Protestantism included a wide diversity of theologies and denominations. These included Presbyterianism, Anglicanism - known as the Church of Ireland - and a range of smaller groupings, of which the most significant was Methodism. Among northern Protestants there was a strong sense of being a 'settler' people. There was an intense belief that since they began to arrive in Ireland during the 17th century, they had 'made good' in their new homeland and that this involved preserving their own distinctive culture.

Those who watched the U.V.F. disembark from their railway carriages in Ballycastle would have seen how well the men were kitted out with weapons, bandoliers, slouch hats and puttees. The residents who watched them parade through the streets to the golf-links for a training exercise would have noted their disciplined marching. Such professional features were not found in every Ulster Volunteer battalion. The Ballymena unit owed a lot to the generous financial support and the military know-how offered to the U.V.F. by prosperous businessmen and British Army veterans in Ballymena. The Young family, owners of the elegant Galgorm Castle, had bankrolled the local Ulster Volunteers and had been prominent in the U.V.F leadership in the county, as plans were made for a provisional government in Belfast.[2] In the event of Home Rule, this body aimed to resist unwanted legislation and to enable Ulster unionists to govern the north of Ireland for themselves. Sir Edward Carson, the unionist leader, had recently described this northern part of the island as the 'Protestant province of Ulster' and all those who followed him had pledged themselves in a document known as the 'Solemn League and Covenant' to protect their interests 'by whatever means necessary.'[3]

On that Bank Holiday Monday, a spell of bad weather affected more than just the sight-seers on board the Princess Victoria. The U.V.F.'s military manoeuvres on the Ballycastle golf-course were soon abandoned and the men were summoned to the Presbyterian Church to shelter from the rain. They sat in the pews, waiting for their homeward train and clutching their Mauser rifles. To help them while away the time until the Ballymena train arrived at the station, the men were given a musical recital by the church organist. Their military hardware had been shipped from Germany to Ireland in April and it was part of a consignment that had been distributed to the U.V.F. throughout Ulster, after most of the cargo had been landed at Larne harbour. The guns had been procured from a Jewish arms dealer in the city of Hamburg.[4]

---

1. For the information about events in Ballymena and the Ulster Volunteer Force trip to Ballycastle, see *Ballymena Observer*, 7 August 1914 and *Ballymena Weekly Telegraph*, 8 August 1914. Regarding the U.V.F. trip see also Philip Orr, *The Road to the Somme* (Belfast, 2008), p 41.

2. The correspondence of Sir Arthur O'Neill, as found in the O'Neill papers in the Public Record Office of Northern Ireland indicates the manner in which the Ballymena battalion of the U.V.F. was financially supported by local business, with Willy Young funding a new order of equipment worth £250, and also trained by experienced officers, with O'Neill himself, as a Boer war veteran, giving military advice to colleagues - see correspondence dated 1, 2 March 1914 (P.R.O.N.I., Arthur O Neill papers, D. 1238/ 9A). See too Chapter Five of Timothy Bowman, *Carson's Army* (Manchester, 2007) for a study of the varied level of financial backing and professionalism in various U.V.F. units across Ulster.

3. Carson's use of the phrase 'Protestant province' came during a speech in September 1911 and is quoted in A.T.Q. Stewart, *The Ulster Crisis*, (London, 1967), p 47. The phrase 'by whatever means necessary' may be found in the wording of Ulster's Solemn League and Covenant.

4. For details of the U.V.F. parade in Ballycastle, see Orr, *The Road to the Somme*, p 41 and *Ballymena Observer*, 7 August 1914. The entire gun-smuggling operation is well covered in Stewart, *The Ulster Crisis*.

Ulster politics before the outbreak of the Great War

If Sir Edward Carson had for rhetorical reasons described Ulster as 'Protestant', he would have known that approximately 690,000 inhabitants of the nine counties in Ireland's northern-most province were Catholic and that the vast majority of Ulster Catholics supported Home Rule just as much as their co-religionists in the rest of the country, seeing it as a part of the age-old quest for Irish dignity and independence. Indeed fifty years previously, Catholics had possessed a slight majority within the Ulster population.[5]

Even in Mid-Antrim, with its intense Protestant heritage, there were a substantial number of Catholic citizens. In one of the three electoral districts that comprised urban Ballymena, nearly a quarter of the inhabitants were Roman Catholics.[6] The nearby Glens of Antrim constituted a nationalist heartland and hosted annual festivals of Gaelic culture, organised and supported by a wide range of sympathetic and 'liberal' Protestants as well as by Catholic enthusiasts.[7]

A large nationalist militia had also been formed throughout the island in the latter part of 1913, known as the Irish National Volunteers (I.N.V.). It was led by the Dublin professor Eoin MacNeill, who hailed from the small town of Glenarm on the County Antrim coast, just a few miles east of Ballymena. During that holiday weekend in August 1914, the County Antrim executive of the Irish National Volunteers met in Ballymena's Catholic Hall. Present at the gathering were representatives of the county's 5,000 strong membership. On the Saturday they passed a resolution demanding that the British soldiers who had shot dead several Irishmen at Bachelor's Walk in Dublin shortly beforehand, should be brought to justice as common criminals. The shooting had occurred as the National Volunteers brought their own more modest consignment of smuggled arms into the country, in answer to the U.V.F.'s gun-running exploits.[8]

Nationalists who opposed British control over Ireland's political, economic and civic life drew on a long tradition of resistance, which had involved periodic outburst of insurrection. In recent decades this had been given a new edge due to the terrible sufferings of the Great Potato Famine, in which hundreds of thousands of Irish men and women had died of starvation and disease despite their existence near the heart of a worldwide and very prosperous empire. Throughout these years of Irish hardship, the Catholic faith had been perceived as a bulwark of support.

In the shadow of such long-standing conflicts, throughout the summer of 1914 fresh battle lines in Ireland were being drawn. The rival citizen armies watched each other with suspicion, even in Mid-Antrim where the U.V.F certainly outnumbered its rivals. The two militias were observed in turn by Ulster's uneasy official peacekeepers, the men of the Royal Irish Constabulary (R.I.C.). As will be substantiated later in this narrative, the County Antrim leadership of the U.V.F. had drawn up maps, on which local divisions of the Ancient Order of Hibernians were marked, along with an estimate of how many men were thought to belong in each branch.

5. The figures for religious affiliation are given in J.J. Lee, *Ireland 1912-85, Politics and Society* (Cambridge, 1990) p 1-2 and are based on a reading of the Census for Ireland 1911 (http://www.census.nationalarchives.ie/search/) (24 September 2010)

6. A breakdown of religious affiliations for the electoral district 'Ballymena Town' as catalogued in the 1911 Irish Census, yields this figure. Of the 4,247 inhabitants, 1,022 were registered as Roman Catholic.

7. For a thorough study of the attempt to revive and celebrate Gaelic culture in the Glens, see Eammon Phoenix et al (eds.), *Feis na nGleann: A century of Gaelic Culture in the Antrim Glens* (Belfast, 2005).

8. The I.N.V. meeting in Ballymena's Catholic Hall is noted in correspondence (Mid-Antrim Museum, U.V.F. archive, during August 1914) and the meeting is also noted in *Ballymena Weekly Telegraph*, 8 August, 1914.

The maps also indicated where the nearest U.V.F. company could be found in the event of civil conflict, when local nationalists would have to be swiftly suppressed. The Hibernians were a fraternal Catholic grouping who were dedicated to the Home Rule cause and supportive of the growth and eventual arming of the Irish National Volunteer movement.[9]

In truth, the stage was being set, in Mid-Antrim as elsewhere throughout the north of Ireland, for a civil war in which much blood was likely to be shed. It is arguable that in both militias, discipline and leadership actually helped to prevent worse disorder from taking place. However, the petty sessions courts in Ballymena and district had heard a number of cases during the summer of 1914 which gave evidence of tension on the streets and several related acts of petty violence.

The court heard how in mid-July, the relationship between two neighbouring families in Alexander Street had burst out into open warfare, with the women particularly involved in hostilities. At this time of year, when the Orange Order paraded on a regular basis throughout Ulster, 'party feeling' was not uncommon. Now that Home Rule loomed, tensions were much greater. In the Alexander Street fracas, lemonade bottles, a baby's 'sucking bottle', fireside tongs, a brush-head and eventually a wheelbarrow were all used as weapons. Windows were shattered in each family's home. One side claimed that they had been abused for their Catholic religion and their nationalist politics, having been subjected to provocation with an unfurled Union flag and a bowl of orange lilies. The other family claimed that a loyal flag had been snatched out of their little boy's hands and that the offending party had threatened to 'stamp on it,' saying she would 'travel in Orange blood.'[10]

As we shall see in this historical account, a number of street disturbances had already occurred in Ballymena by 1914. Property had been damaged, effigies of local citizens had been burnt and extra police had been drafted in to help contain the situation, although no lives had ever been lost in these relatively brief episodes of more serious conflict.

Outbreak of war

The summer of 1914 did not end with the war between unionists and nationalists that many had dreaded in Ulster. That is because 4th August 1914 was no ordinary day. Even as Ballymena went about its business on that Tuesday morning, telegrams were being exchanged between officials in the foreign offices of Europe's most powerful nations. Decades of imperial rivalry had boiled over throughout the summer. The continent stood on the threshold of full-scale war. During 4th August, German troops poured through Belgium on their way to Paris, determined to strike an early blow against their long-term rival, France. In immediate support for its French and Belgian allies, Britain declared that unless the German generals had promised by midnight to withdraw from Belgian soil, a state of war would exist between the British Empire and Imperial Germany.

No such promise was given, and on the morning of Wednesday 5th August, the inhabitants of Ballymena, whatever their allegiance, found themselves involved in a European War. Suddenly priorities would change as both unionist and nationalist leaders in Ireland realised the strategic value of 'rallying to the call' which the government was making for Irishmen to join the British Army. Each side was hopeful of repayment in due

9. (P.R.O.N.I., Arthur O'Neill papers, D. 1238/8).

10. *Ballymena Weekly Telegraph*, 8 August 1914.

course for military loyalty in time of war. The local civil tensions, though far from vanished in the long term, would abate relatively quickly throughout the rest of 1914 as the rival agendas of the U.V.F. and the I.N.V. were put on hold.

European conflict had loomed since Archduke Ferdinand of the Austro-Hungarian Empire had been shot on 28th June by Bosnian Serb nationalists who wished to secede from that empire and join the neighbouring Kingdom of Serbia. Russians and Austrians were long-standing rivals in the Balkans and when Austria went to war with Serbia, Russia was obliged to respond with help for the Serbs, whom they saw as kindred people and valuable allies.

Through the tight system of alliances which prevailed at the time, France was treaty bound to help Russia against the Germans while Austro-Hungary was strategically linked to Germany, which was now a very powerful state, lying at the heart of the continent and jealous of the huge global empires of the other 'great powers'. Germany was already an economic dynamo and it was in possession of a large and very proficient army. Britain, as an ally of Russia and France, did not wish to see its continental interests threatened, so throughout July 1914, as international diplomacy failed to handle international anger, the British government began to contemplate the fearful possibility of involvement in a large-scale European war.

By Tuesday 4th August, most Mid-Antrim men who had had any connection with the British Army knew that they would be summoned back to their old regiments, on the very moment that war was declared. Among those who awaited the call was the local M.P, Sir Arthur O'Neill. Based at Shane's Castle on the shores of Lough Neagh, O'Neill was not only a member of parliament and a key figure within the U.V.F. in County Antrim, he had also been an officer in the famous English cavalry regiment, the Life Guards.[11] Many other more humble citizens of Ballymena and the surrounding district were members of the military reserve, having served at one time as full-time soldiers. Within hours of the declaration of war, they would be expected to make their way to a military barracks.

Many locals, like people in other parts of the British Isles, believed that the European conflict would not go on for long. Among them was the octogenarian John Young of Galgorm Castle, who was the owner of the Braid Water Spinning Mill and Ballymena's biggest employer. The old man doubted that the fighting would last beyond Christmas.[12] However the war would not finish by the end of 1914 and before it drew to a halt in November 1918, hundreds of young men from County Antrim would perish. In the years that followed, the pre-war conflict over Irish governance would resume with much greater intensity.

So how had people in and around Ballymena experienced the years that preceded the First World War? It was a time when local unionists felt proud to belong to a relatively prosperous part of an empire on which 'the sun never set.' It was a time when nationalist citizens were excited by the prospect of a resurgent Gaelic nation, reclaiming its own language, celebrating its own culture and rolling back the tide of a British dominance which they felt had swamped the island of Ireland for far too long. And it was a time when some local people undoubtedly struggled with the pressure to make the choice of one or other of these increasingly opposed allegiances.

---

11. A brief sense of O'Neill's military career - he went on to die in the Great War - is given on a very comprehensive website dedicated to the war-dead of Ballymena, which provides essential material for anyone who wishes to understand the role of soldiers and sailors from Mid-Antrim. (www.snake43.webs.com/weeklywar1914.htm) (July 2010).

12. Eull Dunlop (ed.), *The Recollections of Mary Alice Young* (1867-1946) (Ballymena, 1996), p 53.

Chapter One

Mid-Antrim on the Eve of Change

Chapter One
Mid-Antrim on the Eve of Change

The Mid-Antrim gentry

The conflict between nationalism and unionism dominated the pre-war years in Ulster, yet there were other reasons for social rupture. Not least of these was a class-system in which wealthy landlords and factory owners sat at the top of society and an impoverished working-class at the bottom. Throughout Europe, these were the very differences that led during the second decade of the 20th century to the growth of a strong labour movement and indeed to violent revolutions in some countries, during which inherited status and economic privilege would be swept away. In Mid-Antrim as elsewhere in Europe, a considerable economic distance existed between the top and bottom bands of the social spectrum.

In the early 17th century, the latest attempt by Britain to 'pacify' the Gaelic heartland of Ulster had included the plan to send thousands of Scottish and English settlers across the Irish Sea, where it was hoped that they would bring civic order, the Protestant religion and long-term prosperity to the region. However, those 'planters' from Scotland and England who started settling in County Antrim and who became the dominant cultural force in this part of the island, included few who had come to Ireland to establish vast estates or build palatial houses. There were very few who possessed inherited riches or could lay claim to illustrious family pedigrees. Almost three centuries later, the majority of the really wealthy families in Mid-Antrim owed their position to recent industry and commerce or to professional success.

In the immediate pre-war years, the local solicitor William Shaw wrote and published a short book about the village of Cullybackey, situated five miles to the west of Ballymena. He referred proudly to his home area as 'a neighbourhood of many mansions,'[13] but it is quite clear that the resident families in these 'mansions', while they may have considered themselves to be 'gentry,' were far from being aristocrats. The Young family owned a particularly fine example of 17th century domestic architecture known as *Galgorm Castle*. However, they had purchased it from its previous owner in the mid-19th century as their family started to make good in the textile trade.[14] After their business expanded, they became the owners of other attractive properties, including the country residences known as *Hillhead House* and *Fenaghy House* as well as a 19th century mansion in Ballymena, called *Kintullagh*. At the heart of the Young family's wealth was the huge Braid Water Spinning Mill, which at its peak employed 1,200 workers.

The Fraser family were also thought of as local gentry. They lived in the residential elegance of Hillmount, sharing ownership of the Hillmount factory with the Haughton family who resided nearby. William Shaw noted that their wealth was based on the recent growth of the textile trade which included the 'bleaching and finishing of linens, sheetings, damasks and general household goods.' He remarked on the fact that at the factory 'over 8,000,000 square yards are put through the various processes every year.'[15]

---

13. William Shaw, *Cullybackey - the story of an Ulster village* (Edinburgh, 1913) p 123.

14. Alex Blair, *County Antrim Characters*, volume 1 (Ballymena, 1993) p 7.

15. William Shaw, *Cullybackey - the story of an Ulster village* (Edinburgh, 1913) pp 140-143.

Braidwater Mill, Ballymena

Image 4. The Braid Water Mill was the biggest employer in pre-war Ballymena and it brought considerable wealth and status to its owners, the Young family. (Mid-Antrim Museum collection)

Amongst the other mansion-owners who attracted Shaw's attention were Joseph Skillen of Lowpark, who was the manager of the Phoenix Weaving Mill and Captain John Patrick of Dunminning House, who had a military background. Quite a number of significant Mid-Antrim gentlemen had had a military career. To the east of Ballymena, in the vicinity of Broughshane, the country estate of *Whitehall* was home to a retired professional soldier, Sir George White, who had risen to become a general in the British Army and was a winner of the Victoria Cross, earning his honours for resolute leadership during the siege of Ladysmith in the Boer War.[16]

However, amongst the Ballymena gentry some families did possess a more exalted status. The Adair family owned extensive property in Suffolk and possessed much of the land on which Ballymena had been built over the previous three centuries. By the Victorian period, the Adairs had been elevated to the peerage, having gained the title 'Baronet Waveney.'[17] Just beyond the southern borders of Mid-Antrim, the O'Neill family of Shane's Castle possessed an illustrious pedigree. They had descended from one of Ulster's great 17th century political families, the Chichesters, but they could also claim connection to the famous O'Neill clan, whose leaders such as Shane and Hugh had once spearheaded Gaelic resistance to English conquest. Any real connection with Gaelic clan culture had long since been severed by the time of the Home Rule crisis, however

---

16. Plentiful information on the mansions and gentry of Mid-Antrim in the pre-war era is located throughout Shaw, *Cullybackey - the story of an Ulster village*.

17. Alex Blair, *Mid-Antrim Characters*, volume 1 (Ballymena, 1993) pp 7-11.

on gaining a baronetcy in the mid-19th century, the Chichesters had chosen to re-acquire the O'Neill name, with all its mystic aura.[18]

One other notable family, the O'Haras, had been a Gaelic clan with ancient rights to ownership of large stretches of Mid-Antrim. By the early years of the 20th century, a mixture of adventurous marriages, legal disputes and changes in religious affiliation had led to the dispersal of the family. By the time of the Home Rule Crisis, *Crebilly Castle*, which was the family seat of the O'Haras, had become the prized possession of the Dinsmore family, who had been significant figures in the local textile industry since the 18th century.[19]

By the second decade of the 20th century, several members of Mid-Antrim's industrialist class had donned the garb of culture and achieved landed elegance, as well as enacting their daily role as hard-headed businessmen with a mill to run. John Young's Galgorm estate would have employed a wide range of local people in roles as diverse as gardener, cook and gamekeeper - occupations which would have been standard for a substantial rural property. There were stables and gardens and a working farm. A herd of deer roamed the parkland of over 200 acres. There were pleasant walkways where a busy gentleman might take a walk of an evening, in order to relax after the demands of a day's business affairs.

There was also the obligatory historic ruin at Galgorm, which added romantic allure to the grounds of the castle, in the shape of a rudimentary fort that had belonged to the McQuillans, an Irish clan which had owned the territory in and around Galgorm, during the vanished years of Gaelic lordship.[20] For Willy Young, a son of John and the master of *Kintullagh*, an ideal weekend was spent engaged in such gentleman's pastimes as hare-coursing or shooting game on the hills of Donegal or the moors of the Mull of Kintyre.[21]

For the ladies of the Young family, a life of luxury and leisure was certainly an option. Despite the fact that she was an energetic and highly individualistic woman, Rose, the daughter of John Young, kept a diary that reveals a daily life of great privilege in which most chores were undertaken by the servants, who served up fine meals from the kitchens, as and when required. The gentlewomen of the house seemed to have few major obligations other than to visit their relatives and neighbours, then extend hospitality in turn. Rose Young would certainly have received an invitation to the wedding of one of the Haughton boys in 1912, which was the occasion for a celebration in the neighbourhood. A tasty supper was provided by the Haughton family for a socially mixed gathering which included the workers at the mill who had collected money to buy 'Master Sam' a gift. A crowd gathered around a celebratory bonfire, lit on a nearby hilltop, as the festivities continued into the night in a scene which at first sight indicates a social harmony quite undisturbed by the disruptive forces of 20th century modernity.[22]

18. Information on the O'Neill family is located in R.M. Sibbett, *On the Shining Bann*, (Ballymena, 1991) p 143-144.

19. Interview with Brian O'Hara, *Ballymena Family History Society* (15 February 2011).

20. Information about the Galgorm estate can be gleaned from (Mid-Antrim Museum, the Young photographic collection, see, for instance, photographs of farming activity, the walkway to the McQuillan 'fort' and the resident herd of deer).

21. For information on Willy Young's pastimes see Dunlop (ed.), *The Recollections of Mary Alice Young*, p 45 and the diary of Rose Young, August 1913. Rose Young's diary is an abbreviated version of a much more detailed and personal document which the writer unfortunately destroyed. It is on loan from a private collection to the Mid-Antrim Museum.

22. *Ballymena Weekly Telegraph*, 28 September 1912.

Image 5. Crebilly Castle, which was originally the home of the O'Hara family. By the time of the Home Rule Crisis, ownership had passed into the hands of the Dinsmore family, seen here. The Dinsmores owned a number of textile factories throughout Mid-Antrim and one family member, John Dinsmore, was a Liberal in his politics and an opponent of militant unionism. (Mid-Antrim Museum collection)

The working class

This was the era of 'upstairs/ downstairs' servant culture, a period when young working-class men and women still presented themselves at the twice-yearly hiring fair in Ballymena, keen to find work and board.[23] Not just the gentry but the more prosperous farmers, merchants and professionals in Mid-Antrim all kept servants, although hiring fairs in towns like Ballymena were primarily for the acquisition of agricultural labourers. Domestic employment was also obtained through responses to advertisements or by tapping into a local network of informal community acquaintance. The pay was fairly meagre and tenure was often temporary and dependent on obedience to the master or mistress. However, the various roles on offer, whether as 'yard man' on a large farm or as a maid in the home of a doctor or solicitor, did offer a degree of security and status. This was important in an era that was still without an extensive social security system, even though the Liberal government at Westminster was in the process of trying to create new networks of insurance and social welfare.

The presence of servants in the house often brought Protestant home-owners in Mid-Antrim into contact with Catholic men and women, invariably from a broadly nationalist background, who presented themselves,

---

23. Information on Irish hiring fairs is located in May Blair, *Hiring Fairs and Market Places* (Belfast , 2008).

alongside Protestants, at the local hiring fairs. Many people in the vicinity were seemingly happy to hire, train and lodge their servants, irrespective of religion and politics, if they looked like effective and reliable employees. John Young set an example, while exercising leadership within the ranks of the exclusively Protestant Orange Order. In 1911, four Catholic servants resided at *Galgorm Castle*.[24]

Image 6. Rock View, Ballymena, also known as Flag Lane. It was a cul-de-sac of stone houses. Hundreds of Ballymena citizens lived in cramped housing such as this. (Mid-Antrim Museum collection)

However, life at the bottom of the social scale was far from secure for Protestant and Catholic alike. The Ballymena Workhouse, managed by the local Board of Guardians, would have prided itself on caring with strict but charitable concern for those who were at the social margins and had neither fixed abode nor a sustaining family network. As in almost every Irish town, there were some thoroughfares which had a special reputation, whether fully deserved or not, for poverty and cramped housing. One such place was Alexander Street.

Many of the homes which had been built in Alexander Street were erected during the previous century and were certainly an improvement on what had gone before but they were still cold and damp in winter and could be stiflingly hot in a summer heat wave. There was a single upstairs room, known as 'the laft', where several children and their parents slept with a blanket hanging from the ceiling as the room's only partition. A sense of privacy was very limited.[25]

In some houses on Alexander Street, migrants from various parts of Ireland were packed into the upstairs

24. Census for Ireland 1911 (http://www.census.nationalarchives.ie/search/) (24 September 2010).

25. Interview with Debroy Barr, Ballymena (12 February 2011), who recalls members of his family describing the living conditions.

and the downstairs rooms, irrespective of the rival religious affiliations that mattered so much in the conflict which by 1914 was threatening to tear Ulster apart. As indicated earlier in this narrative, fierce rows between Catholic and Protestant residents in Alexander Street and in other working-class parts of the town did surface from time to time but the Ballymena police would seem to have been more frequently employed in dealing with generic 'drunk and disorderly' behaviour, which was a common reaction to the harsh conditions experienced by working-class communities at this time. Although one advertisement in *Ballymena Observer* extolled the virtues of a brand of whiskey which 'drives away the heartache and substitutes no headaches', the stark realities of misery and addiction were observed on more than one occasion by R.I.C. constables who found men lying prostrate in the Ballymena streets, with an empty bottle of methylated spirits at their side.[26]

Migration from the Ulster countryside to provincial towns such as Ballymena and to the much larger urban area of Belfast was a popular option due to the availability of routine work in mills, and factories. Many rural areas in Ulster had experienced a population decline during the first decade of the 20th century, due to emigration as well as local urbanisation. Whereas the population of Ballymena town had grown by nearly 5% since 1901, the rural Ballymena district had seen shrinkage of 12%, the most dramatic drop in numbers within the entire county.[27] By 1911, the houses in many of Ballymena's thoroughfares had filled up with men who sought a job in workplaces such as Kane's Foundry and with men and women, boys and girls who tried to gain employment in the Braid Water Mill and in other mills and factories.

Some of these thoroughfares had nicknames. Alexander Street had earned the unofficial title 'Clabber Street', 'clabber' being an Ulster expression for muck or dirt. The word may have been somewhat apt, given the proximity of the nearby Ballymena market and the use of the street as a route by those who led their livestock there to be sold. However, the grim implication was that the inmates of this street were unclean.

A substantial number of the Ballymena working-class resided in an area to the south of the River Braid, which was developing its own regional pride and strong community spirit even though the inhabitants also lived in cramped housing and worked long hours at monotonous jobs for modest wages. By 1911, this adjunct to Ballymena was a network of densely packed streets which constituted a labour depot for industry and was known simply as Harryville, although to some of the residents of 'old' Ballymena, Harryville was referred to as 'Sodom', which may have been in reference to apocryphal gossip about the debauchery that supposedly went on there![28]

Although government reforms had abolished the worst forms of child labour by the 1900s and technical advances had resulted in safer working conditions, an employee in a Ballymena mill could expect to work long hours each day, with only a short break for lunch and as little as 9 shillings' weekly wage for their labour. Children often started work at twelve years of age. Long hours were worked and very modest wages were received by employees at the various bleach greens, flax mills, dye works, scutch mills, woollen weaving mills and other workplaces that formed a part of the busy local textile industry, not only in Ballymena but also in

26. For information on the inhabitants of Alexander Street see the Census for Ireland 1911 (http://www.census.nationalarchives.ie/search/) (24 September 2010). For details of the poverty and lack of opportunity experienced by some of the residents see George Elliot, *The Tearaway of Clabber Street*, a locally published account of growing up on this street by a local man, a copy of which is kept in the Local Studies section of Ballymena Library. Details of 'rowdyism' including alcohol abuse in the district are readily available from a reading of the petty sessions records in both local papers during the years 1911-14. See, for example, *Belfast Weekly Telegraph*, 23, 30 September, 28 October 1911, 23 March 1912.

27. The local census figures for rural and urban population change were presented and discussed in *Ballymena Weekly Telegraph*, 24 August 1912.

28. Harryville is referred to as Sodom in recollections by a senior Ballymena resident in Eull Dunlop (ed.), *John Luke's Harryville* (Ballymena, 1992) p 7.

smaller Mid-Antrim settlements such as Connor and Cullybackey. Considerable variations in wages between the different employers would cause friction during the pre-war period.[29]

Farmers, merchants and rising prosperity

The flax from which linen is made was grown locally by County Antrim's farmers, many of whom also kept pigs, sheep and cattle which were sold at the Ballymena market. Some farmers grew potatoes and vegetables to be sold in Ballymena's wide range of food shops or else they planted cereal crops, which were in demand for the production of bread, animal feeds and whiskey.

Many farmers relied heavily on the linen trade, growing several fields of flax and 'retting' it in their own flax dam. Then they would take it to the local scutch mill, where the long process of turning the plant into a textile would begin, or else they sold it to dealers at the Ballymena market.

The farming community in the heart of Mid-Antrim was mainly Presbyterian in affiliation and during the previous decades these farmers had been the beneficiaries of land reform, which saw ownership pass out of the grip of the landlord class and into their own hands. They then experienced growing prosperity because the industrialisation of Ulster had created adjacent markets for their produce. As Ballymena was well-connected to Belfast by railway line, the area's agricultural products could be shipped to the city with ease. Pig, beef and dairy farming were especially popular.[30]

A merchant class and an artisan class had developed in the heart of Ballymena, providing both basic and luxury products and important everyday services to a burgeoning class of prospering farmers and to those families which were involved in managing and profiting from the textile trade. The pages of the two local papers for this period, *Ballymena Observer* and *Ballymena Weekly Telegraph*, show a range of businesses which had sprung up during the early years of the 20th century in order to cater for the needs and wants of a type of citizen who had some money to spend, whether in temperance tea rooms, 'drug halls', spirit merchants, motorbike sales rooms, drapers' shops or - in the event of a loved one's sad demise - a monumental mason's workshop, specialising in such materials as Sicilian marble. Advertisements for Kane's Foundry portrayed a range of equipment for sale with which to maintain the success of local agriculture, including 'haycarts, threshing and churning machines, mowers, reapers...rakes and binders' all to be viewed in the showroom on the Waveney Road.[31]

Despite the thousands of local residents who lived in poverty and were employed in laborious and ill-paid jobs, Ballymena and district was developing a reputation for solid middle-class wealth, for business acumen and for a prudent hold on any recently acquired financial resources.

There was a growing prospect of modest wealth for those in Ballymena and district who were skilled and who possessed aspirations. And there was every likelihood of a small but reasonably steady daily wage, even for

---

29. Debates between rival employers about local wage rates in the Mid-Antrim textile business are presented in correspondence published in *Ballymena Weekly Telegraph* during October and November 1913 - see for instance John Dinsmore's letter to the editor, 6 November 1913.

30. For information on agriculture in the hinterland of Ballymena at the beginning of the war-years, see an unpublished and un-dated study made of *Ballymena during the Great War*, P.S.H. Frazer, Ballymena 1914-18, which is kept in the Local Studies section of Ballymena Library. See in particular, p 26.

31. For the Kane's Foundry advertisement see *Ballymena Weekly Telegraph*, 2 March 1912.

Image 7. A thriving middle class had developed in Mid-Antrim by 1911. Commercial life was growing, in keeping with much of the rest of Edwardian Britain, leading to a wider range of luxury goods in local shops. Lancashire's chemist shop had a mineral water business at the back of the premises. (Mid-Antrim Museum collection)

those who could aspire to little else than work on a factory floor. As a result, the blatant social inequities of early 20th century Britain would appear to have gone largely unchallenged in Mid-Antrim in the years before 1911. The labour unrest that was becoming more widespread in urban areas throughout Britain and Ireland and much further afield seems to have made relatively little appearance in the district. The contagious creed of socialism appears to have possessed little appeal thus far.

It is worth noting that the Catholic community within Ballymena produced a number of bright economic success stories. One of the key figures in local business life was Patrick Murphy, who owned a vibrant soft drinks manufacturing business as well as participating in the liquor trade. One of his beverages gained a prestigious award at a food and drinks fair in Paris, which would have proven to local unionist ideologues that a man could rise socially and achieve prosperity in a community like Ballymena, whether he attended a Protestant or a Catholic place of worship. As a consequence, endangering the status quo through Home Rule agitation would have been deemed an inappropriate and unwise political response from local Catholics.[32]

---

32. *Ballymena Weekly Telegraph*, 6 April 1912.

Unionist culture and devotion to the Empire

For most of those Protestant citizens who held key roles in Mid-Antrim society, their stability, freedom and prosperity was guaranteed by one thing more than any other. This was the position of Ulster near the very heart of the British Empire. Belonging to this empire had not prevented Ireland from experiencing a terrible mid-19th century famine. However, that was not considered a valid reason amongst Ballymena unionists for expressing any doubts in the empire's virtues. According to a set of racially coloured Victorian values which still endured in much of Britain, such a disaster was probably due to the lassitude and backwardness of the 'native' people rather than any failure of policy. The rank administrative inadequacy which helped turn the potato blight into a massive human catastrophe would not have been lamented in unionist circles in Ballymena. The destruction of the Gaelic peasant way of life in Connacht and Munster during the famine years and during subsequent decades of mass-emigration was not something which local unionists attributed to cold-hearted colonial maladministration nor was it something that they felt obliged to mourn, as firm believers in social and economic 'progress' away from a 'backward' existence towards a 'modern' one.

The city of Belfast, lying thirty miles to the south of Ballymena, seemed the perfect demonstration of what the south and west of Ireland should have been capable of. It was fast-growing and dynamic and for some people at least it was a very prosperous city. Its shipyards built glamorous liners and its manufacturers exported goods everywhere that the Union flag flew, from Canada to Australia. The textiles which Ballymena produced also had a worldwide market and high-quality linen was regarded as the 'queen of fabrics'.

Image 8.
Empire Day in Galgorm village involved the custom of saluting the Union flag. This day provided a holiday from school for local children and presented unionist leaders with a chance to instil patriotism within the young.
(Young Collection, Mid-Antrim Museum)

Empire Day was a recently established annual event throughout Britain's worldwide domain, during which local children were encouraged to find out more about the achievements and values of the British peoples. On Wednesday 24th May 1911, on a day of fine, bright weather, Galgorm village adjacent to the Young estate was draped in red, white and blue bunting as John Young's son George addressed a crowd of local people, reminding them that they belonged to 'the greatest empire the world had ever seen' and assuring them that the people of Galgorm would always be safe if they 'stuck truly to that flag.' The Ballymena Temperance Brass Band marched through the village as did a recently founded troupe of local scouts. Then a meal was provided for everyone in the Young Memorial Hall, due to a generous provision of festive food by members of the Young family.

Pupils from the local National School sang a number of songs and there were recitations from the works of Rudyard Kipling, the bard of empire.[33] Amongst the poems which the school-children of Galgorm would certainly have been encouraged to learn by heart was one entitled Recessional, written by Kipling for the diamond jubilee of Queen Victoria in 1897. It was a piece of verse which celebrated the empire but also warned the British people that without vigilance, their empire could crumble, just as other empires had done in bygone times:

'God of our fathers, known of old –
Lord of our far-flung battle line
Beneath whose awful hand we hold
Dominion over palm and pine –
Lord God of hosts be with us yet,
Lest we forget, lest we forget...

If drunk with sight of power we loose
Wild tongues that have not thee in awe-
Such boastings as the Gentiles use,
Or lesser breeds without the law –
Lord God of hosts be with us yet,
Lest we forget, lest we forget...'

In the following month came another opportunity to celebrate the power and wonder of Britain. Although King Edward VII had died the previous year, the coronation of the new monarch George V did not take place until Tuesday 22nd June 1911, which was, unfortunately a day of rather mixed weather in County Antrim. However, an artillery salute resounded from the ground opposite Ballymena Town Hall and a massed choir stood and sang a version of the Hallelujah Chorus, which had been in preparation for several months. The gentry, the businessmen and the public officials of the Ballymena area were invited to a lunch in the Town Hall and a large Union flag was unfurled from the Adair family's castle walls, an event which was greeted, in the words of one local newspaper, by 'the exultant cheers of the Loyalists of the district.' Then, despite the occasional rain-shower, 2,000 local children were served tea in the Ballymena Demesne under the shadow of the castle. The boys and girls had all been given medals and banners to mark the occasion.

According to Ballymena Observer, after dusk the weather was sufficiently dry for a fireworks display to

33. Ballymena Observer, 26 May 1911.

Image 9. The proclamation of the accession of George V in Ballymena. Boys of the Church Lads' Brigade are present as are the Royal Irish Constabulary. A rift between the police and unionists would open up as the Home Rule crisis developed. The Ulster Volunteer Force eventually made plans to seize local policemen, in the event of a loyalist coup d'etat. (Young collection, Mid-Antrim Museum)

take place and for a 'magnesium bonfire' to be lit on the 'castle tower'. Many houses throughout the town had been decorated with bunting, flags and portraits of the new monarch and prizes were handed out for the best decorated homes. Ballymena residents had been encouraged to place a lamp or candle in their window throughout the hours of darkness and a 'fire balloon' was also lit and sent into the sky to hover over the Braid Valley. Further east, the celebrations were also underway. On top of Slemish mountain, a huge bonfire was now visible across much of Mid-Antrim.

Braid Water Mill was one of several workplaces which had been decorated with banners and bunting in the course of the previous week. The most eye-catching feature of the display was a large illuminated crown which incorporated the letters G.R., standing for 'Georgius Rex', and the familiar, loyal words 'God Save the King'. On top of the building, a Union flag floated in the breeze.[34]

---

34. *Ballymena Observer*, 16, 23 June 1911.

Protestant and Catholic cultures in Mid-Antrim

In July and August came the usual round of summer celebrations by the Protestant fraternal bodies known as the Loyal Orders, which possessed a strong presence in Mid-Antrim, both in long-settled rural areas and in newer urban districts such as Harryville. The summer season in and around Ballymena was dominated by Orange Order parades and church services and these celebratory yet solemn events played an important part in reminding local people of the role that the Protestant faith had exercised in establishing their distinct identity and boosting the communal morale of their ancestors. The Orange Order's celebrations were focused on the victory of William, Prince of Orange at the Battle of the Boyne in 1690, when the new English monarch had begun the process of establishing a more effective and secure Protestant regime throughout Ireland.

Most local Protestants thought of themselves as loyalists, not just because of 17th century victories but because they saw themselves as loyal to the values, emblems and leadership of Britain's worldwide 20th century Protestant empire. At a religious service in Ballymena's First Presbyterian Church on 9th July, the Reverend Thomas Haslett preached a sermon to the Orangemen who had marched there from the Protestant Hall on the Galgorm Road. Haslett reminded his hearers that 'the greatest bond of Empire is a common faith' and that that faith was Biblical Protestantism.[35]

A list of local 'lodges' and 'chapters' from the period reads as colourful evidence of the depth of faith-based loyalism. It includes such names as Moyasset Purple Star, Ballymena Golden Star, Moneydig Bible and Crown Defenders and Burnside Royal Arch Purple. Orange culture had started to flourish in Ulster in the late eighteenth century although Presbyterians, as a more marginal 'dissenting' denomination, would not have been admitted to Orange ranks for several more years. Orange rituals in Ballymena were supplemented by commemorations organised by allied Protestant fraternal organisations such as the Royal Black Institution and the Apprentice Boys of Derry.[36]

Clergymen in the main Protestant denominations were mostly members of these Loyal Orders and acted as their chaplains and spiritual champions. As this account will reveal, some of the most vigorous loyalist clergy were to be found in Church of Ireland parishes in outlying villages, including men such as W.H. Lee, who had been recently installed as the rector in Ahoghill and O.W. Clarke, who was the rector in Connor. At Lee's installation, Bishop d'Arcy of the Down and Connor diocese, took a key role in the service. D'Arcy, who was originally from Dublin, had ministered in the Ballymena district as a younger man and he retained close relations with the Young family.[37]

Presbyterian clergy such as Reverend Gilmour of Ballymena's Wellington Street Church were respected ecclesiastical figures with considerable influence on civic life. Although Bishop d'Arcy and a number of other unionist clerics in the Church of Ireland would not have described themselves as evangelicals, most of the local Presbyterian clergymen would undoubtedly have done so. They used this term to emphasise a Christianity rooted in a deep personal conversion experience rather than the sacraments.[38]

---

35. *Ballymena Observer*, 14 July 1911.

36. The pages of *Ballymena Observer* and *Ballymena Weekly Telegraph* throughout the years 1911 -1914 are filled with accounts of lodge meetings, parades and loyalist demonstrations. See *Ballymena Weekly Telegraph*, 22 February, 6 September 1913 for some of the lodges mentioned here.

37. Details of Lee's arrival in Mid-Antrim and of the friendship with Bishop d'Arcy are to be found in the diary of Rose Young, 28 July 1911. See also *Ballymena Weekly Telegraph*, 8 July 1911 and Dunlop (ed.), *The Recollections of Mary Alice Young*, p3.

38. Andrew Scholes, *The Church of Ireland and the Third Home Rule Bill* (Dublin, 2010) p.28.

Presbyterian clerics were especially proud of the spiritual heritage of the 1859 Evangelical Revival, which had originated in the vicinity of Connor and Kells and had swiftly spread across County Antrim and then further afield. As will become clear in the course of this book, the Protestant clergy of Mid-Antrim also tended to be vociferous opponents of Catholicism.

Image 10. The Congregational Church in Kinhilt Street, Ballymena. A range of smaller Protestant denominations existed in Mid-Antrim, including Baptists, Reformed Presbyterians and Moravians. (Mid-Antrim Museum collection)

Since the days of the Reformation, there had been a long tradition of opposition to the Roman Catholic church in British political and religious life. Texts such as the famous Foxe's Book of Martyrs had played a significant part in the evolution of British Protestant culture. This eighteenth century book described in graphic detail the torture and execution of Protestants by a Catholic Church that regarded them as heretics, during the years that followed the Reformation. Vivid woodcuts showed Protestant families being burned at the stake and Catholic priests torturing heretics in order to make them recant. In the self-confident and increasingly urbane environment of Edwardian Britain where Catholics were a relatively small minority, the fears acknowledged and stirred up by such books had largely receded. In Ireland, where Catholics were a pious majority and saw themselves as a politically disenfranchised but resurgent group of people, religious fears among Protestants were very prevalent.

In the bleak aftermath of Ireland's mid-century potato famine, Archbishop Desmond Cullen had risen to power within the Irish Catholic church and played a key role in stirring piety and devotion, encouraging high levels of respect for parish priests and arguing the case for church control of education. What is more, in 1870 he had been one of the dominant figures in the Vatican's formulation of the doctrine of papal infallibility, by means of which a more centralised and uniform Catholic church aimed to flourish worldwide.[39] Faced with an Irish nationalism that was harnessing the reserves of global Catholicism to facilitate new forms of Irish self-respect, many Protestant clergy were frightened of the consequences for their 'flock' and for their own social status. They feared that a large-scale resurgence of Irish Catholicism was unstoppable and that it would involve severe attacks, motivated by resentment of the long years of Protestant institutional privilege in Ireland. Many clergy thought the advance of Catholicism would involve the widespread promulgation of theological error and the growth of papal authoritarianism.

Although information on the Catholic community within Ballymena and its hinterland is much harder to obtain, it is clear that the Catholic population of the town numbered just over 2,000 by 1911. It is also obvious that Catholics in County Antrim had been hit by the mass-emigration that was such a prevailing feature of Irish rural life since the Great Famine of the 1840s but that ongoing urbanisation had led to a steady growth of the town's Catholic population, up from 1,616 in 1881. The All Saints Catholic chapel on the Cushendall Road was a grand and impressive place of worship, built in 1860 under the influence of a dynamic parish priest called Father Lynch. More recently, a fine new parochial house had been constructed under the leadership of Canon O'Donnell, who had arrived in the town two years earlier. A breed of confident and articulate Catholic citizens was emerging in and around Ballymena. Many of these men and women found companionship and stimulation in the Catholic Reading and Debating Society, which met regularly in the Catholic Hall.[40]

The growth of civic life in Ballymena

Civic life in Ballymena was flourishing. The town had several venues which played host to theatre performances, often organised by the popular impresario, Payne Sneddon. There were cinema shows in the Ballymena Picture Palace on a nightly basis, and there were craft, art and furniture displays in the Protestant Hall, involving the very latest in leather work, ceramics and china, lace, metalwork and household furniture. And there were now two golf courses on the edge of town as well as a number of other sports clubs. Sport was modish and popular and the new rector of St Patrick's Church of Ireland was a keen 'rugby man' and his wife was an enthusiastic golfer.[41]

Elocution teachers were busy in Ballymena, preparing local young people for the circuit of speech and drama competitions in Ulster towns. Both classical and popular concerts were a regular feature of the social scene. A number of local bands performed in public in the summer months, such as the Ballymena and Harryville Young Conquerors and the Ballymena Temperance Brass Band, while the Ballymena Minstrel Troupe performed in such venues as the Church of Ireland Parish Hall, offering their audiences the latest 'negro classics' such as *The Old Folks At Home* and *Poor Old Joe*. On other occasions, displays of Scottish dancing took place, including the

---

39. For detailed information on Cardinal Cullen see Desmond Bowen, *Paul Cardinal Cullen and the shaping of modern Irish Catholicism* (Dublin, 1983).

40. For statistics of Catholic religious affiliation in Ballymena, the author has analysed the Census for Ireland 1911 (http://www.census.nationalarchives.ie/search/) (24 September 2010). Urban Ballymena had approximately 11,500 inhabitants in 1911, of which slightly over 2,000 were Catholic. See *Ballymena Weekly Telegraph* during March and November 1911, for occasional articles information about meetings of the debating society. See also information contained in the locally published Fraser, *Parish of Kirkinriola - a historical sketch* (1969) an anonymous pamphlet available within the Local Studies section of Ballymena Library. This short document possesses no specific authorship and would appear to have been published under the auspices of the local Catholic parish for consumption by parishioners. It offers a very broad history of the Catholic community in Ballymena up to the 1960s. The Debating Society mentioned here will be referred to and referenced at a later juncture in this chapter.

41. Information on local theatre, cinema, arts and crafts and sport may be found at many locations in local papers. See for instance *Ballymena Weekly Telegraph*, 11 October, 24 November 1911, 29 March, 1913.

Image 11. Galgorm Road, Ballymena - one of several smart, handsome thoroughfares that seemed to present good evidence that Mid-Antrim was thriving under the Union. (Mid-Antrim Museum collection)

popular *Highland Fling*. There were several well-attended evenings of fancy dress by young pupils who had been trained by two local teachers, the Misses Millar. The Y.M.C.A.'s gymnastic classes were a popular diversion for local young people. New youth organisations such as the Scouts were well-supported and teams from the Church Lads Brigade went to rifle shooting competitions in Belfast and came back with prizes.[42]

Despite the interest in 'good elocution' amongst the local middle classes, there was a proud sense of distinct linguistic identity in Ballymena and district, in which pronunciation and vocabulary owed much to the Scottish ancestry of many of the local people. The editor of *Ballymena Observer*, John Wier - who proudly possessed a variant on the usual spelling of his surname - wrote a humorous weekly column in his newspaper, which he composed in an Ulster Scots dialect under the nom de plume 'Bab McKeen'.

The poet Thomas Given was one of several local scribes who followed in the tradition of County Antrim's 'rhyming weavers' and celebrated the local landscape in a distinctly Scots idiom, if with some florid touches:

---

42. Information on dance, music, elocution and youth activities may be found for instance in *Ballymena Weekly Telegraph*, 19 April, 1912, 19, 26 April, 3 May 1913.

'Hear me ye nymphs, sae aften seen
Frae Hillmount House tae Lowpark Green,
Shud beauty ever want a Queen
Its throne to share,
In safety we may lift our een
An' crown her there...'[43]

Image 12. Mill Street, Ballymena, with a view of the Old Town Hall where both the Urban and Rural District Councils met. Legislation in the previous century had resulted in the creation of a tier of local government in Ireland where local businessmen and landowners could often wield considerable influence. (Mid-Antrim Museum collection)

Should anyone wish to retire to a local hostelry to read Given's poems or peruse the thoughts of Bab McKeen, there was an array of venues which offered sustenance. This included the plush and comfortable Adair Arms Hotel and the newly opened Seven Towers Tea Rooms in Mill Street, which advertised its 'cleanliness and promptitude' and claimed that 'meat teas' were its most tasty speciality.

The Ballymena Races were popular each Easter, bringing flocks of visitors to the town, as did the Ballymena Home Industries Fair in the autumn. Modernity was also evident in the number of streets being resurfaced with tar macadam instead of the traditional cobbles. Modernity was also present in the much-welcomed

43. From the poem *By the Maine*, quoted in Shaw, *Cullybackey - the story of an Ulster Village*, p 183.

arrival of a skeletal telephone service. Ballymena Technical College was growing from strength to strength and now had 500 students. Ballymena Academy and Cambridge House schools both sent academically gifted students each year to further or higher education, in such institutions as Trinity College in Dublin and Queen's University in Belfast, both of which were now open to young women as well as male students.

There was a growing interest throughout the district in medical matters and in public health. The Cottage Hospital, on the edge of the People's Park, provided help for those who could not afford to pay large sums for independent medical care but were not so lacking in resources that they had to plead for free assistance at the dispensary in the local workhouse.

The Mid-Antrim Nursing Society took a deep interest in all things to do with the health of the district, delivering lectures and creating 'travelling displays' about the perils of tuberculosis. Within individual religious denominations, a lot of work was done to care for the needy. A Catholic Ladies' Association of Charity flourished in the town, relying on voluntary labour. Inside Protestant circles, the Band of Hope endeavoured to tackle the issue of alcoholism, as did the organisation known as the Pioneers inside the Catholic denomination. Other temperance and abstinence groups such as the Rechabites, the Good Templars and the Catch my Pals had a presence in the district.[44]

So in the eyes of many of its citizens, as the second decade of the 20th century got under way, Ballymena and district was a thriving, settled and peaceful area.

However, there was compelling evidence of radical change. From the viewpoint of Galgorm Castle or the Ahoghill Rectory, that change did not look good.

Cottage Hospital, Ballymena.

Image 13.
The Cottage Hospital was seen as proof of the town's social progress. It would be supplemented by the new, larger Waveney hospital during the period of the Great War. (Mid-Antrim Museum collection)

44. The pages of the two local papers during the period 1911-14 carry evidence of most of the civic events, activities and institutions noted in this chapter. See too the Belfast and Province of Ulster Directory (1905) for references to local nursing and healthcare. Information on commercial and civic life may be found in the Belfast and Ulster Towns Directory (1910). See also a scholarly, unpublished study, Fraser, P.S.H., *Ballymena 1914-18*, which contains information germane to the immediate pre-war years and is found in the local studies section of Ballymena Library. The Seven Towers Tea-room was advertised in *Ballymena Weekly Telegraph*, during April 1913. At the end of each year, reports on academic successes at the two main secondary schools in the town featured prominently in local papers.

Ballymena in an era of growing industrial unrest

Daily newspapers carried evidence that many of the industrial workers on whose toil Britain's wealth depended were no longer prepared to accept the wages and conditions that their employers stipulated. In 1907, a strike had taken place in Belfast in which a wide variety of union members took industrial action on behalf of the city's 3,000 dockers, some of whom were working a 75-hour week with no real employment rights. The strike united hundreds of Catholic and Protestant workers in common cause, under the leadership of the charismatic labour activist, Jim Larkin and was only broken up after a form of martial law was imposed in the city.[45]

Throughout 1911, strikes were a familiar part of the British industrial landscape. A transport strike in Liverpool resulted in Mid-Antrim's meat exports sitting on the quayside in Merseyside, due to the absence from work of the local dockers.[46] Strikes also took place that year in Glasgow, Wales, London and Cumbria. Railway strikes and bakery strikes occurred in Dublin and though they ended in failure for the strikers, there were signs that the Irish unions were starting to organise themselves more skilfully and that leaders such as the charismatic Jim Larkin would try again to test the strength of employers against the power of organised labour.

There were several contemporary British working-class activists who came from a background which devout Mid-Antrim Protestants could have endorsed. The Labour M.P. Keir Hardie had grown up in a humble Scottish Protestant home and honed his oratorical skills as an evangelical preacher, skills he would put to use in the cause of Welsh strikers in 1911, where he proclaimed his willingness to support the men in 'a fight to the finish.'[47] An Independent Orange Order had been established in Ulster in recent years, ostensibly to give expression to a loyalism which was more favourable towards labour issues, but it showed little sign of adopting socialism or modifying its highly charged Protestant rhetoric. In any case it possessed less strength in Mid-Antrim than it did further north, in a region in and around Ballymoney which was known as The Route.[48]

Then labour unrest hit Ballymena in 1911 and it undoubtedly caused deep worry in Galgorm Castle and the other 'mansions' of Mid-Antrim. Despite the sketchy coverage of the unrest in local papers, it is clear that a disruptive strike began in the Braid Water Mill on 25th January. Over 150 'doffers' and 'layers' had recently applied for extra wages due to an increased workload brought about by the installation of new machinery. They proclaimed that they had had absolutely no response from the management to this request. According to *Ballymena Weekly Telegraph*, the workers in question then 'paraded through the streets for several hours, singing popular airs' and assembled at the mill-gate at 5.30pm. The police were summoned to maintain order.

A newspaper report on Saturday 28th January indicates that as a result of the disruption to normal spinning procedures, the other workers at the mill were now idle and no less than 1,200 employees were without work. The industrial action continued for some days, with local newspapers eventually reporting on 11th February that the strike had been settled.

A prolonged lay-off at the town's largest place of employment would certainly have made a big impact on the

---

45. Details of the strike are located in John Gray, *City in Revolt - Jim Larkin and the Belfast Dock Strike of 1907*, (Belfast 1985).

46. *Ballymena Weekly Telegraph*, 18 August 1911.

47. This statement by Hardie is quoted in *Ballymena Weekly Telegraph*, 26 August 1911.

48. The Independent Orange Order has not been thoroughly documented by historians but more information about the group may be found at www.Iloi.org (November 2010).

lives of those who depended on it for a weekly wage and caused local factory owners a degree of real alarm. However, because of the failure - and perhaps the unwillingness - of local newspapers to cover the story in depth and due to the lack of archival material relating to the mill's governance, the role of the unions, the strategy of the employer and the attitude of the workforce, details of this strike are not at all clear. It may be argued that John Wier, the editor of *Observer*, was a significant figure in the golden circle of Ballymena's top businessmen and probably reluctant to give 'the oxygen of publicity' to the strikers. Clearly such challenges to the industrialists who owned the mills and factories of Mid-Antrim presented a threat to the social unity needed in any concerted Protestant campaign against Home Rule.[49]

The Young family would also have looked with alarm at strike actions in neighbouring towns. In Ballyclare, just a few miles south-east of Ballymena, a strike took place in mid-August at the paper mill. The workers had been trying since June to have their union recognised by the employers and they were keen to discuss the issue of wages and the problem of obligatory 'Sunday labour'. The action persisted until mid-September and their union supported the workers financially until the issues were resolved. An agreement was only reached when employers met with union leaders from England, who pressed for 'reinstatement of workers without victimisation, the conduct of future negotiations through the union officials and the company officials, advances in wages as per June application and abolition as far as possible of Sunday labour.' The prospect of negotiating with union leaders who were operating at this level of status and effectiveness would have troubled the minds of all Ballymena industrialists.[50]

Image 14. Sir Arthur O'Neill became the local M.P. in 1910. He is seen canvassing in Henry Street in Harryville, with George Young on his right. The Orange arch has been painted with supportive slogans. Despite this portrayal of an aristocratic parliamentarian in his local fiefdom, economic unrest would soon rise to the surface in Mid-Antrim and industrial action would become common. (Mid-Antrim Museum collection)

49. *Ballymena Weekly Telegraph*, 28 January, 4, 11 February 1911.

50. *Ballymena Weekly Telegraph*, 19 August , 16 September 1911.

Local women in the era of the suffragettes

However, other social changes were in the air. The suffragette movement was rarely out of the news, as it continued its campaign for votes for women. In the north of Ireland, acts of civil disobedience and arson attacks by militant suffragettes took place throughout the pre-war years. One woman from the County Antrim seaside resort of Whitehead, called Margaret Robinson, gained notoriety for smashing windows during a protest in Piccadilly in central London.[51] Even those women who were at the heart of the Mid-Antrim 'establishment' were intrigued by the suffragettes and Mrs Fraser, in the unionist redoubt of Hillmount, would eventually host a meeting to discuss the issue of emancipation.[52] Suffragette activists appeared in Ballymena town-centre, advertising their open-air meetings by writing the time and place in chalk on the pavements and roadways. On one occasion, the female campaigners stood in Broadway and addressed the gathering crowd, only to be 'heckled' by several young men who made loud comments about the attractive qualities of one of the women and subsequently followed them towards the railway station, 'playfully' mocking their views.[53]

Young ladies who had been brought up in the privileged environment of the 'big house' were more likely than most to read widely and to travel beyond the geographical confines of Mid-Antrim, thus exposing themselves to a radical perspective on the constrictions traditionally experienced by women. By 1911, several ladies from within the Ulster gentry had already rebelled against the social norms and cultural preferences of their families, including County Antrim women such as Ada McNeill and Margaret Dobbs. Added to this number was Rose Young of Galgorm. For a number of privileged Ulster Protestant women, female independence found its expression not so much in active suffragette politics as in a deep and often controversial commitment to the Celtic Revival. In some of these women, the commitment extended to a passionate advocacy of Irish Home Rule.[54]

Rose Young was a keen student of the Irish language and she taught classes in the subject. She signed herself in correspondence as Rois ni Ogain and attended Irish-speaking cultural events in Belfast organised by the Gaelic League. She participated in the running of the Glens Feis (or 'festival') along with a number of other Ballymena citizens, where the Irish language and Irish history, customs and mythology were given pride of place. Rose Young acted as a marker in the Feis's Irish language essay competitions and she presented prizes to the winners, some of whom came from Ballymena, where Irish language classes had grown in popularity, including one class which had begun to prosper in Harryville. Amongst her tutorials on Irish culture was a 'Round Tower' lecture, which focused on the architectural glories of Celtic Christianity.[55]

---

51. *Ballymena Weekly Telegraph*, 16 December 1911.

52. Fraser, *Ballymena 1914-1918*, p.11.

53. *Ballymena Weekly Telegraph*, 7 September 1912.

54. For extensive information on Ada McNeill, Margaret Dobbs and Rose Young see many references in Phoenix, *Feis na nGleann*, including an article by Fred Heatley, 'The Woman Revivalists'.

55. Information on Rose Young and local classes in the Irish Language and culture can be found in her diaries throughout the period 1911-1914. For example, her 'Round Tower' lecture took was noted on 24 February 1910 and her Irish language teaching on 3 November 1913. See too a series of reports on the Irish Language in the local newspapers, for example *Ballymena Observer*, 9, 30 June 1911 and *Ballymena Weekly Telegraph*, 14 January 1911. See also *Irish News*, 7 July 1913. For wide-ranging information on the topic of Irish see Phoenix, *Feis na nGleann* and also Roger Blaney, *Presbyterians and the Irish Language* (Belfast, 1996).

The growth of nationalist self-confidence in Mid-Antrim

An Irish language class which met at a school room on the Cushendall Road was accompanied by regular Sunday night history classes, taken by Father Bradley. There were frequent ceilidhs where four hand reels and Irish jigs were danced with great enthusiasm. In the repertoire of those who sang at concerts in the school room, such pieces as *The Harp that once through Tara's halls* by Thomas Moore were great favourites. Also in the repertoire was *The West's Asleep* by Thomas Davis, with its evocation of the wild beauty of the Atlantic coast and its plea for Irish freedom:

> 'That chainless wave and lonely land
> Freedom and Nationhood demand.
> Be sure the great God never planned
> For slumbering slaves a home so grand...
>
> Sing, Oh, Hurrah! Let England quake.
> We'll watch till death for Erin's sake.'[56]

The task of renewing the Irish language in County Antrim was a challenging one. By 1911, it had more or less died out as an everyday language, even in the Glens. As will become clear however in this account, a number of members of the Royal Irish Constabulary who were stationed in and around Ballymena were perfectly capable of communicating in Irish. These policemen often came from the west of Ireland, where the native language had survived longer than elsewhere.

Rose Young's great challenge was to combine the unionist ethos of Galgorm Castle and the Celtic mystique of the Antrim Glens. The speeches made by her friends at venues such as Cushendall, Glenarrif or Garron Tower on the beautiful Antrim coast, were very different from the ones delivered by her father and brothers, a few miles inland on the unionist platforms of Ballymena. In the last few days of June 1911, just as loyalists were moving happily on from the coronation of George V to the annual '12th July' celebrations of the Battle of the Boyne, a crowd came to the Glens for the annual Feis. During the celebrations they assembled at a hilltop cairn which was dedicated to the memory of the 16th century Ulster clan-chief, Shane O'Neill, who had gone into

Image 15. Taise Banner carried in the opening procession of the first Glens Feis of 1904. It was one of a set designed by John Campbell (Seaghan Mac Cathmhaoil). (Ballycastle Museum collection)

---

56. *Ballymena Weekly Telegraph*, 25 March 1911.

battle against the powerful armies of the Tudor monarchy. The Belfast antiquarian Francis Joseph Bigger made a stirring speech at the cairn and reminded his hearers that on days such as this they were all very proud indeed to be 'Gaels and Irishmen.'

A reporter for *Ballymena Weekly Telegraph* who was at the Feis noted how 'prizes for the prettiest blouses of Irish material worn on the day' were presented to several young women. A Miss Mary Miller and a Miss Madge Logue from Ballymena were both included on the list. Amongst other activities was a hurling match between a team from Belfast and one from the Glens. The teams that played these Irish 'traditional' games were often named after ancient Irish warriors such as Cuchullain or Fionn and his Red Branch Knights. Each year at the Feis, there were displays of Irish 'traditional' costume and Irish dancing and there were competitions in which children were challenged on their knowledge of Irish history. Although few explicit detailed avowals of Home Rule politics would have taken place at the Feis in 1911, nonetheless the organisers were motivated by a desire to recover a primal cultural identity that they felt the many years of colonisation by Britain had almost extinguished, thus delivering a much less rosy picture of the British Empire than the one which was promoted during recent coronation ceremonies in Ballymena Demesne.[57]

For one close relative of Rose Young, the Feis had already been influential in stirring up fervent Irish patriotism. This was the talented diplomat and humanitarian, Roger Casement, who, several years before, had come to Ballymena as an orphaned child and experienced the care of his relatives in the Young and Casement families, who sent him to the school that would later become known as Ballymena Academy, for his early education.[58]

It was also obvious to Mid-Antrim unionists that Gaelic revivalists were at ease with Catholicism and that some of the Feis's greatest supporters were Catholic clergy and prominent Catholic lay people. This easy intermingling of a resurgent Irish identity and Roman Catholicism was a worrying development for those Protestant citizens of Ballymena who had been brought up in the long-standing if fading British ecclesiastical tradition which regarded the Roman Catholic Church as heretical, dictatorial and superstitious.

Recent Catholic teachings seemed dangerous to Ulster's unionist leaders and opinion-formers. Several significant Irish church leaders pointed out the role of the worldwide *Ne Temere* decree issued by the Vatican in 1908. This had stressed that a marriage ceremony which was not performed by a Catholic priest lacked legitimacy. The ruling also inferred that any couple who were married 'legitimately' must definitely promise to bring up their children as Catholics. Bishop d'Arcy declared that in the event of Home Rule, this ruling would cause a conflagration.[59] In 1910, a brother of the Ballymena lawyer John McCann had become the subject of a news-story when he left his Protestant wife, taking his children with him and declaring that the marriage, which had not been celebrated by a Catholic priest, was null and void. Not surprisingly, a strident critic of the *Ne Temere* decree was the Ballymena clergyman who had originally married McCann, the Reverend Gilmour of Wellington Street Presbyterian Church.[60]

---

57. Both Ballymena newspapers during the summer of 1911 carry reports on the Feis. See *Ballymena Weekly Telegraph*, 1, 8 July, 1911.

58. There are numerous books and articles that throw light on the life and significance of Casement. For a relevant and detailed examination of Casement's life and his local connections, see Geoffrey Dudgeon's study of the sexually graphic private diaries which Casement kept through a substantial part of his adult life - Geoffrey Dudgeon, *Roger Casement - The Black Diaries* (Belfast, 2002).

59. J.J. Lee, *Ireland 1912-85, Politics and Society* (Cambridge, 1990), p 11.

60. Evidence that the original McCann marriage had been celebrated by Gilmour is located in the proceedings of a legal case dealt with later in this account and covered in depth in *Ballymena Weekly Telegraph*, 2 March 1912.

Historians have also pointed to deep fears in Ulster Protestant circles about a recent papal ruling - known as 'Motu Proprio' legislation - which seemed to condemn Catholics to ex-communication if they dared to take a legal case against a member of their clergy in a court of the land. This ruling appeared to augur poorly for civil and religious liberty in an Ireland where the Irish Parliamentary Party would hold the majority in a Home Rule parliament. The prominent Presbyterian, lay figure, Thomas Sinclair, spoke of his fears that in a era of growing clerical authority the 'liberty of speech and voting' among nationalists would be suppressed by the Irish Catholic church and the nationalist voter would be 'under the absolute control of their hierarchy.'[61]

Meanwhile, the sentiments being expressed at the Catholic Literary and Debating Society in Ballymena, offered a clear indication that the age-old dream of an autonomous Ireland was alive and well amongst local Catholics. At one meeting in the 1911 season, congratulations were offered to a young member called John Doherty who had been promoted within the insurance company for which he worked and was now moving on a permanent basis to Belfast. Those members of the society who offered Doherty their congratulations spoke of his great successes as a public speaker and recalled a particular occasion when he had delivered an impassioned talk in Kilrea Town Hall on the subject of Daniel O'Connell, whom he referred to as 'Ireland's Great Liberator' because of his victory in the struggle for Catholic Emancipation during the 1820s and his subsequent attempt to gain repeal of the Act of Union which had dissolved the Irish parliament in 1801.

Another speech by Doherty was fondly recalled during the course of the evening. On that particular occasion he had spoken in Rasharkin on the topic of Robert Emmett, who had been executed for his leadership of an unsuccessful insurrection in 1803. Doherty referred to Emmet as 'one of Ireland's most noble sons.' On the farewell night for Doherty, one speaker went on to hope that the young insurance worker might one day advance in the use of his oratorical skills to the point where he would be 'pleading his country's cause in parliament.' In his reply, John Doherty, who had not been born in the area, was complimentary about the friends he had recently made in Mid-Antrim, saying that 'amongst the sterling Nationalists of Ballymena he had found nothing but kindness.' He believed that:

> 'the cause in which they had been associated for some time was marching to a triumphant end, at a pace sufficient to make everyone most hopeful.'

This was unquestionably a reference to the Home Rule project. Doherty hoped that he would soon be able to 'come back and toast the success and prosperity' of a 'newly-formed Irish parliament' in Dublin. And he concluded by praising the great courage of Ballymena's 'isolated Nationalists.' Then everyone stood to their feet and sang the anthem God Save Ireland:

> 'God save Ireland say the heroes
> God save Ireland say we all
> Whether on he scaffold high
> Or the battlefield we die
> Oh what matter if for Ireland dear we fall.'

Such hearty and ebullient Irish patriotism was no doubt quite worrying to the unionist burghers of Ballymena and district, even though the debating group were prone to winding up their meeting with toasts not just to

---

61. Sinclair's verdict on the implications of the *Motu Proprio* controversy is cited in Lee, *Ireland 1912-85, Politics and Society*, p 11.

'Ireland a Nation' but also to 'the town and trade of Ballymena'.[62]

From 18th century republicans to opponents of Home Rule

In an earlier era, when Ulster Presbyterians were still not integrated into a modern pro-Union project, many of them had been deeply influenced by the egalitarian rhetoric of the French Revolution. Numerous County Antrim Presbyterians had given their allegiance to the revolutionary body known as the United Irishmen and Ballymena had been, however briefly, a republican stronghold during the insurrection of 1798. It was a year which had left behind a range of vivid stories and legends in the district.

William Shaw, the Cullybackey historian, reminded his readers that the pillars of Fenaghy House had once been topped by ornamental lead figures in the era when the McManus family had lived there. In 1798, the lead had been carried away by rebel soldiers in order to make bullets. Subsequently:

> 'the local leaders of the United Irishmen met to discuss the plan of campaign in the large ice-house…and as it was directly opposite the strong room in which the family plate was kept, Mr McManus, fearful lest they would make as free with the silver as they had with the leaden men, destroyed the house.'

Such acts of insurrection had not disturbed the calm environs of Cullybackey in the intervening years. Many Presbyterians had turned their backs on a separatist project that had been so bloodily crushed by the British government. Protestant 'dissenters' were now becoming part of the 'mainstream' within political and civic life throughout the British Isles and local Presbyterian leaders such as Henry Cooke advocated close links with this 'mainland' culture. Local Presbyterians had been welcomed during the nineteenth century into the ranks of the Orange Order and many of them had imbibed a form of Victorian evangelicalism which either allied itself strongly with the British Tory party or else sought a local form of British Liberal Party politics which rejected the Home Rule ideals of the Victorian premier and Liberal leader, William Gladstone.[63]

Meanwhile, the famous pike-men who had fought in 1798 had become part of the political heritage of an Irish nationalism that possessed a distinctly Catholic flavour, as evidenced by the current Irish patriotic motto 'Faith and Fatherland'. By 1911, the faith thus alluded to was assumed by most local citizens to be of a Catholic variety. Stories of atrocities committed by Catholics against Protestants in the south-eastern county of Wexford during 1798 had circulated, occluding the enlightenment optimism with which numerous late 18th century Presbyterians had once embraced revolution and reintroducing earlier planter fears of massacre and dispossession.

In the wake of 1798, the Irish parliament had been suspended and the safety of Ireland from rebellion had been bolstered by direct government from Westminster after the Act of Union in 1801, when Irish MPs were obliged to represent Irish constituents as a minority group in 'the mother of parliaments.' Constitutional nationalism sought to bring about Irish freedom through the campaigns of the Irish Parliamentary Party in London rather than through insurrection. It had become a strong advocate of the national cause in the latter decades of the nineteenth century and had helped win over the British Liberal Party to the project of re-instating a 'Home Rule' parliament. This kind of Irish parliament was thought by some English politicians to be

62. See *Ballymena Weekly Telegraph*, 11 November 1911, which contains details of the farewell event for Doherty. On 25 March 1911, in the same paper, there is further evidence of the toasts given at the Debating Club.

63. Shaw, *Cullybackey - the story of an Ulster village*, p130-131.

an institution that would satisfy Ireland's hunger for dignity, while maybe lessening the urge to break away completely from the British Empire, fragmenting the Union which lay at its heart.

William Gladstone's Home Rule Bills of 1886 and 1893 had not been passed but the new Liberal administration which came to power in 1906 was convinced of the need to create fresh Irish legislation and by 1910 it depended on the support of Irish nationalist MPs when passing laws through the House of Commons. In 1893, it had been the House of Lords which rejected the 2nd Home Rule Bill although the Commons had accepted it. Now, amidst a plethora of reforms, the Liberal Party was passing a Parliament Act which was due to become law in the summer of 1911.

This act would cripple the power of the 'upper house' to block a bill, meaning that controversial legislation could only be held up by the Lords for two years.

As the Liberal government now planned an initial reading of a 3rd Home Rule Bill in the Commons during 1912, this meant that Ireland would soon have a parliament in Dublin for the first time in over a century. It was a parliament that would possess only limited executive powers, nonetheless it was a legislature which Ulster unionists believed would be subject to the domination of Irish nationalists and the economic needs of the poorer, pre-industrial and heavily Catholic southern counties. It might also be the first dangerous step along a road to complete severance from Britain.

Radical change was looming and Ulster's unionist leadership was agreed that something radical must be done to prevent it.

Image 16. Proclaiming the accession of King George V at the Old Town Hall in Ballymena in 1910, with Willy Young speaking. In the following year, Coronation Day was also celebrated. The British Crown attached to the wall, was one of several emblems which were illuminated at night. (Young collection, Mid-Antrim Museum)

First unionist reactions to the 3rd Home Rule Bill in Mid-Antrim

In reaction to earlier Home Rule threats, Unionist Clubs had been set up throughout the north of Ireland, where the Protestant population was a dominant or at least a significant force. There had been some military drilling and an interest in the acquisition of arms. The clubs had lost momentum in the period after 1893 but by the time the new Home Rule crisis loomed, they were being reformed, mentored by the Ulster Unionist Council which had been created in 1905.

In March 1911, Captain Hall from Narrow Water Castle in County Down arrived at Galgorm. He would appear to have been tasked by the Unionist Council with helping local leaders put the Ballymena Unionists Clubs into good working order. He had come to the right place. John Young was too old to offer the energy needed for the job but his sons Willy and George were both keen and they felt capable of taking on the challenge. The clubs needed either to be resurrected or newly formed at smaller towns such as Ahoghill and Broughshane and within Ballymena itself, at a location in Harryville and in the 'North End' of the town.[64]

A large public meeting was due to be held in September at Craigavon, the Belfast estate of Captain James Craig, much of whose family wealth had been earned in the whiskey business and who had seen military service in the Boer War. Ulster's men and women were asked to gather as one and show their support for a massive, extended campaign to block the proposed Home Rule legislation. Mid-Antrim's Unionist Club members were of course welcome to come to Craigavon. The meeting would be addressed by Sir Edward Carson, the eloquent, high-ranking lawyer and Westminster MP, who was becoming the public figurehead of the anti-Home Rule cause.

Throughout the summer of 1911, as Unionist Clubs began to awaken and plans for participation in the Craigavon mass-meeting started to take shape, the note of political alarm was being sounded at loyalist parades in Mid-Antrim. At one local '12th of July' Orange demonstration, a Church of Ireland clergyman, the Reverend O.W. Clarke warned of the 'economic disaster' that he believed Home Rule would bring. Conscious of the historic precedent of Irish nationalists siding with Britain's international rivals and wartime enemies, one other speaker, Andrew Kennedy, warned that if there was a war with Germany 'Nationalists would take the side of the Germans' as they had taken the side of the Boers during the recent South African Wars. Sir Arthur O'Neill M.P., of Shane's Castle, who had actually served in the Boer War, took to the platform and suggested that under Home Rule, the nationalist leader John Redmond would become their prime minister, at which a very loud voice in the crowd added 'and the Pope...'[65]

In late August, Belfast members of the 'Black' institution came to Ballymena for their annual parade. The unionist M.P. William Moore addressed them and declared in no uncertain terms that Home Rule would be 'disastrous to the Empire and ruinous to Ireland.' He noted the strikes which were paralysing the transport network in Britain and declared that the Liberal government's reaction to the disruption was 'weak as water and as mild as milk'. So he wondered what would happen if 'loyal Ulster went on strike' in order to gain 'freedom from Nationalist oppression' and to obtain release from the 'traitors who wished to place their neck under the heel of the Vatican.'[66]

---

64. Diaries of Rose Young, 8 March 1911. See too *Ballymena Observer*, 1 March, 1912.

65. *Ballymena Weekly Telegraph*, 15 July 1911.

66. *Ballymena Weekly Telegraph*, 2 September 1911.

Such statements became frequent as unionist fears intensified in the months that lay ahead. Several speakers stirred their audiences by describing the 'likely' fate of Ulster Protestants under Home Rule and depicting the resistance which they felt unionists should offer to nationalist 'treachery'. At a meeting in Ahoghill Orange Hall in September, a 'Brother Nevin' employed vivid rhetoric as he strove to convince his hearers of the need to 'keep the banner still unfurled that so many traitors were trying to pull down'. He referred darkly to John Redmond as the leader of a 'Romish clan' which every Protestant would one day have to oppose through the force of arms. In that grim event, promised Brother Nevin 'every man will grasp his musket, spear or sword before we yield to Popery.'[67]

Such warnings sounded a familiar note in loyalist oratory. Although mass-murder of the descendents of Ulster's 17th century settlers had not taken place in County Antrim since William III established the 'Protestant Ascendency' in the 1690s, nonetheless a folk memory of an earlier rebellion in Ulster in 1641 was often invoked in Orange culture. In this episode, thousands of Ulster planters had died as the Catholic and Gaelic population of Ireland had risen up in an attempt to 'retrieve their land' and then, as the rebellion went on, to seek vengeance for their loss.

Meanwhile, groups of men from the district's Unionist Clubs prepared to join the crowds at Craigavon, under the supervision of the Young brothers and aided in their plans by Sir Arthur O'Neill of Shane's Castle. Protestant unity was needed. This would involve scotching the rumour that a number of County Antrim Presbyterians were still infused with the spirit of 1798 and might not be behind the unionist project. *Ballymena Observer* carried an article on 22nd September, in which severe doubts were expressed about the ability of the Ulster Liberal Association to rally any Protestant support whatsoever for the Government's Home Rule Bill. The U.L.A. contained men who admired the British Liberals and still held a torch for the reformist Irish policies of Gladstone's heirs, which had included extensive land reform. However a 'Liberal Unionism' that opposed Home Rule had become a great deal more popular among Ulster's instinctive Liberals.

The letter-columns of *Observer* carried missives in which the rumour that numerous Presbyterian clergy were 'home rule sympathisers' was immediately dismissed -some nationalist politicians had recently been inclined to argue that there was considerable Presbyterian clerical sympathy for their cause. In September, *Observer* also took note of the recent growth of the Ancient Order of Hibernians and carried reports that it was a very dangerous 'separatist' organisation. Such articles indicate this newspaper's important role as a purveyor of pro-Union sentiment, a role that reflected the political loyalties of its owner, John Wier, who was an active unionist.[68]

At Craigavon in September, the leaders of the Mid-Antrim Unionist Clubs witnessed an inspiring sight. Tens of thousands of fellow-Protestants from all across Ulster carried Union flags and anti-Home Rule banners and listened with rapt attention to the defiant words of Carson, who stated quite emphatically that unionists would set up their own provisional government rather than submit to rule from Dublin. Particularly impressive on the day, were a number of Unionist Club members from other parts of Ulster who paraded in and out of the Craigavon grounds in military fashion.

---

67. *Ballymena Weekly Telegraph*, 29 September 1911.

68. For details of the opposition to pro-Home Rule Presbyterians, details of local Liberal politics and criticisms of the local Ancient Order of Hibernians , see the pages of the local papers. For instance *Ballymena Observer*, 1, 22 September 1911, 12 January, 2 February 1912. For John Wier's membership of his Unionist Club see *Ballymena Weekly Telegraph*, 7 December 1912.

As they returned to Mid-Antrim, it would have been clear to John Young, his sons and his political colleagues that as influential businessmen and gentry they must play a role in the creation of a command structure for the evolving Ulster unionist campaign. It would also have been clear that they should build a more militant unionist presence in the Ballymena area. This would involve military training for Unionist Club members, profiting from the army background of a number of local men who were committed to the cause. These gentlemen included the eminent Ballymena lawyer Robert Orr, who had spent a recent period of his life in British Army uniform. The support and expertise of the retired general Sir William Adair would be invaluable. He lived at Dunadry, some distance to the south of Ballymena but he would be the ideal person to take on a leadership role within the county. His family connections with the town would make him a popular leader there. Sir Arthur O'Neill's participation in the Boer War seemed to indicate his suitability for training and leading men.[69]

Given the power of the rhetoric employed by the platform speakers at Craigavon and the way in which the large crowd had been so deeply stirred, it also seemed important to organise public meetings throughout Mid-Antrim, during which the case against Home Rule could be put to the public with fire and vigour, utilising the eloquence of those men who were most familiar with the regular practice of oratory, the local clergy.

To the excitement of Ballymena's unionist leadership, Sir Edward Carson was scheduled to arrive at Ballymena on 26th September, on his way to Portrush. Carson was undertaking a tour of Ulster, aimed at widening the support for his parliamentary campaign against the impending Home Rule legislation. When his train eventually pulled into Ballymena railway station, he got out of his carriage, walked along the platform to the sound of applause from the waiting crowd, then shook hands with John Young and other leading loyalists. A document had been prepared, signed by local Orange figures and by the town's councillors, proclaiming the devotion of Ballymena to the cause. It was handed over to Carson who delivered a short speech in which he assured the audience that 'Ulstermen have never yet failed and never will fail.' He told them that he would lead them in this 'death struggle against Home Rule'. Then he re-entered his carriage and the train steamed north towards the seaside resort of Portrush, with further short stops at Cullybackey, Ballymoney and Coleraine.[70]

Local unionist rhetoric and the beginning of organised resistance

During the winter of 1911-1912, some basic military training was certainly taking place within local Unionist Clubs, inspired by the Craigavon meeting and by Carson's subsequent visit to Ballymena. This was evidenced by the 'goodly muster' and 'soldierly appearance' of the 'Ballymena contingent' which was noticed by journalists when the men made an appearance at Balmoral in Belfast during the large Easter demonstration of 1912.[71] The precise legal issues pertaining to any local community which wished to engage in drill or to carry weapons were unclear in pre-war Britain. The government, while perturbed by Unionist Club activity across the north of Ireland, did not feel able to make a clear or resolute move to stop the military training that was starting to take place.[72]

---

69. For information on the Craigavon meeting see Stewart, *The Ulster Crisis*, pp 40-50. Information about the leading personnel now involved in the development of a local anti-Home Rule movement will play a substantial role in this account (Mid-Antrim Museum, U.V.F. archive). Adair, Orr, Young and O'Neill also make a regular appearance in local newspapers, 1911-14.

70. *Ballymena Observer*, 29 September 1911.

71. *Ballymena Observer*, 12 April 1912.

72. For details on the legal problems related to placing a curb on military training by loyalists see Bowman, *Carson's Army*, pp 30-38.

To the Orange Order, this programme of improvised militarisation did not seem like an alien phenomenon. The Order had had its origins amidst inter-communal conflicts in the County Armagh countryside during the 18th century. Its marching traditions reflected the participation of loyalists in pro-government yeomanry units, which had been used either to suppress or to discourage outbreaks of rebellion in bygone years.

Intense political speech-making became more prevalent, even when these orations were delivered at relaxed, celebratory occasions. At a social gathering of the Orange Lodge L.O.L. 805, in a room within Harryville Mission Hall during late October, George Young, who was acting as the Grand Master of Ballymena District, delivered a forthright and stirring anti-Home Rule speech. The night was also enlivened by 'songs, readings and recitations.' There was plenty of 'tea, cake and pastry' for all and a 'liberal distribution of fruit' before the happy evening came to its customary end with a singing of the National Anthem.[73] A combination of musical entertainment, high politics and drill was also present when the North End Unionist Club moved into their new premises in Linenhall Street and one of the highlights of the first evening was a mandolin solo by a local virtuoso.[74]

Image 17. Ballymena Castle, one of the residences of the Adair family. The Ulster Volunteer Force commander in County Antrim was Sir William Adair. The castle lay at the heart of Ballymena Demesne and formed the backdrop to numerous unionist parades and rallies. (Mid-Antrim Museum collection)

73. *Ballymena Observer*, 3 November 1911.

74. *Ballymena Weekly Telegraph*, 26 April 1913.

One regular feature of the autumn season in Ballymena was a range of 'Gunpowder Plot' services or lectures, held in various churches and halls in early November, during which thanks was offered to God for the delivery of Britain from Guy Fawkes' infamous plot to blow up the Houses of Parliament, during the reign of James I. On 3rd November, *Observer* noted the solemn words with which Orange Lodge L.O.L. 707 always commemorated the capture and execution of Guy Fawkes and his co-conspirators. The Orangemen in this lodge always thanked God for 'the gracious deliverance of the Protestant parliament from the intended Popish massacre by gunpowder.'[75]

Several other themes became the subject for public talks, all of which were meant to awaken local citizens to the fresh threat that seemed to be facing them. On Tuesday 14th November, Reverend William Patterson travelled from Belfast to deliver a lecture in the Y.M.C.A. hall on 'the Boys of Derry, the Prince of Orange and Home Rule.' Patterson inspired his audience with descriptions of how the town of Derry had once stood out against Irish rebel forces. He described the glory of the British Empire and he went on to describe Scotland, England and Ireland as a 'trinity of countries in unity,' which had been designed by God as the nucleus of that 'vast empire', and had brought wealth, civilisation and the Christian faith to impoverished, backward and heathen people all over the world.

The speaker went on to warn against the follies of Irish Home Rule, using words borrowed from the Christian marriage ceremony, saying 'what God hath joined let no man put asunder.' And then he spoke of the exemplary tradition of the 'Christian warrior' who is ready to fight and die both for his country and for his faith. 'Multitudes have died' he said 'fighting for the heavenly King...and have sealed their testimony to the truth with their blood.' The speaker suggested that such sacrifices might soon be needed once again, here in Ulster.[76]

Other talks which were delivered in Mid-Antrim during the winter of 1911-1912 focused on the virtues of William III, the Prince of Orange, who was depicted as an exemplary 'Christian warrior'. At Connor Protestant Hall a stirring lecture on the 'Life and Principles of William III' was given by the Reverend H.C. Wilson of Kells.[77] Meanwhile, local newspapers carried stories about the arrival in India of the new King and Emperor, George V. One article dwelt on a great church service that had been held in Delhi, when the Bishop of Madras told his hearers that 'he held the firmest belief in his Majesty's divine authority.' This article also described the Queen's visits to Delhi's hospitals, during which she had apparently cheered the sick and the needy of that huge city. To Ballymena's unionists, such news was sublime evidence that they were joined to a powerful world-wide political system which was doing God's will on earth.[78]

Other articles, scattered here and there on the pages of local newspapers, told a more disturbing story. *Telegraph* carried an article in December which dealt with proceedings at the petty sessions in the town of Portglenone, on the western edge of the Mid-Antrim district, where there was a confident nationalist presence. The magistrates heard how 'Home Rule' and 'No Home Rule' crowds gathered at weekends in the town or in the nearby villages, especially after the pubs shut down. They often shouted 'party expressions' at

75. *Ballymena Observer*, 10 November 1911.

76. *Ballymena Observer*, 17 November 1911.

77. *Ballymena Observer*, 24 November 1911.

78. *Ballymena Observer*, 15 December 1911.

one another, sometimes exchanged punches and occasionally attacked policemen who endeavoured to break up the confrontations.[79]

Image 18. A local anti-Home Rule postcard from the period. Portrayals of King William III and Queen Victoria appear on the drums. The figures in this scene are wearing Orange sashes rather than the modern-day collarettes. (Mid-Antrim Museum collection)

Image 19. A pro-Home Rule postcard from the period. This postcard features Ireland personified as a woman raising the standard for Home Rule. (Item on display at Mid-Antrim Museum - on loan from Linenhall Library)

Here was fresh evidence that many Irish people who lived in the vicinity did not wish to cleave to the Empire with all the enthusiasm manifested by unionists. Bitter conflict between the two groupings almost certainly lay ahead. In the minds of both unionists and nationalists, preparations to defend the Union or to secure the passage of the Home Rule Bill would have to be stepped up.

---

79. *Ballymena Weekly Telegraph*, 16 December 1911.

Chapter Two

1912 - The Year of the Covenant

Chapter Two
1912 - The Year of the Covenant

Image 20. Lower Bridge Street, Ballymena. The gates of the Braid Water Mill can be seen, through which over a thousand workers came and went on a daily basis. (Mid-Antrim Museum collection)

The local growth of Presbyterian unionism

As part of the fresh impetus being given to local loyalism, a Unionist Club was formed in Glenwherry on 5th January. Then four days later, J.H. Campbell, the M.P. for Trinity College Dublin, was invited to visit Ballymena in order to speak at the Protestant Hall. He chose to focus on an ever popular topic, the unionist assertion that papal and priestly control over the life of the individual Catholic interfered with modern democratic citizenship.[80]

In Ballymena, as elsewhere in Ulster, the month of January was preoccupied with a renewed attempt to consolidate Presbyterian opposition to the Home Rule legislation. A general meeting of the denomination

---

80. *Ballymena Observer*, 12 January 1912.

was held in Belfast on 1st February and it was attended by clerics and significant lay persons from Mid-Antrim. In order to stir up local sentiment, the Ballymena Presbytery had already convened a public meeting on 28th January. The local clergy were there in force and Reverend E.F. Simpson spoke first, arguing - as his colleague William Patterson had done in the previous year - that God had placed England, Scotland and Ireland together for an express spiritual purpose and so these nations must never be pulled apart. Reverend Thomas Haslett also spoke out against 'Protestant home rulers' and re-using an image from the Old Testament story of Jacob and Esau, he declared that they were intent on selling their 'birthright' for 'a mess of Roman Catholic Nationalist pottage.' Although no names were mentioned, undoubtedly members of the audience thought of Reverend J.B. Armour of Ballymoney. His vigorous support for the Home Rule legislation was well known, even if that was a fairly rare phenomenon among the clergy. Haslett ended his oration with the stirring call 'One God, one King, and one country!'

Other Presbyterian laymen joined the clergy on the platform including the lawyer and secretary of Wellington Street church, James Clarke. Clarke spoke in black and critical terms about the Irish Catholic's 'subservience' to the Vatican and then asked his audience how Ulster Presbyterians could ever 'expect tolerance from people like that.' He fervently hoped he would never see the day when 'descendents of Knox and Calvin' were 'placed under the heel of Rome.'

George Bellis J.P then delivered a short history lesson on contemporary nationalism, arguing that it had its origins in the insurrectionary violence of the 19th century Fenian Movement and fearing that nationalists would be content with nothing less than the absolute end of Britain's control over Ireland. Samuel Hood J.P. then referred to Scottish Presbyterian heroism in the face of religious persecution during the 17th century. He painted a vivid picture of the heather on the moors which had been 'stained purple by the blood of the martyrs' during the era of the Scottish Covenanters, who had refused to yield up their 'reformed' faith and religious freedom for any man. A subsequent article in *Observer* referred to the 'pleasing' number of working class men who turned up to hear the speakers at this meeting. He suggested that these ordinary men were now more aware of 'the urgency of the hour'.

Reading the local paper, Ballymena Protestants were also able to inform themselves of the success of the Belfast Presbyterian meeting, where in a vote on the topic of Home Rule only 43 of the denomination's 1,100 representatives failed to express their disapproval of the Liberal Party's legislation. The Presbyterian convention in due course issued a statement in which they declared that there was no course open to them but:

'to stand together as did their Scottish forefathers in the covenanting days and take all means which honest, God-fearing men may avail themselves of in order to defeat this sinister and baneful policy...'[81]

Throughout the month of February, further loyalist meetings were held in Mid-Antrim. The Ballymena District of the Orange Order organised a gathering on the second of the month, with over 1,000 men in attendance. A resolution was passed, offering complete support for the leadership of Sir Edward Carson in the 'trying' days that lay ahead. Several of the members who were present on that evening would have recalled the words of Reverend Haslett at the recent Presbyterian convention. Haslett had praised the eloquent efforts of Carson and suggested that 'in the full light of the New Testament...one ought to say...that is the sort of thing that

81. *Ballymena Observer*, 2, 16 February, 1912.

Image 21. Church Street, Ballymena, with a cow being walked to the market. Ballymena was still very much a market town, at the heart of an agricultural district. (Mid-Antrim Museum collection)

redeems the world.'[82]

But Ballymena's Presbyterians were also aware, through articles and letters which appeared in *Observer*, that support for the anti-Home Rule cause amongst evangelicals and religious non-conformists across the Irish Sea was not always guaranteed. In mid-February, *Observer* printed a letter from a Dr Horton, who claimed to represent Presbyterians, Methodists and other free churches in England and Wales, in which he explained that Irish Home Rule was in accordance with 'the principles of self-government in which we as Free Church men have been reared.' Horton stressed that 'political justice' must lead to changes in the constitution and then, somewhat unhelpfully, he suggested that if Irish Protestants were unhappy with the prospect of a Dublin parliament, they could always relocate to Britain.[83]

Such sentiments may have disappointed Ballymena's unionists but they spurred the leadership, in County Antrim as elsewhere in Ulster, to make fresh efforts to advocate their cause on the other side of the Irish Sea. Sir Arthur O'Neill and other unionist MPs were soon heavily involved in a campaign to win the hearts and mind of all those British citizens who cherished the empire and did not wish to see its cultural and legislative unity come under threat. Support for Ulster unionism was especially high in the ranks of the Tory Party.[84]

---

82. *Ballymena Observer*, 9 February 1912, *Ballymena Weekly Telegraph*, 3 February 1912.

83. *Ballymena Observer*, 16 February 1912.

84. See Patrick Buckland, *Irish Unionism, 1885-1923* (London, 1973) for details of the unionist campaign in Britain.

The dilemma for Liberal Party supporters in Ballymena

Not surprisingly, for members of the Liberal fraternity in Mid-Antrim who belonged to the local 'Reform Association' there was now a quandary to be faced. Devoted to the values of the British Liberal Party and reluctant to embrace a Tory party that they identified with 'landlordism' or a local politics coloured by aggressive religious disputation, most members nonetheless felt deeply uneasy about the Home Rule project and in particular about the pro-Home Rule meeting that the Ulster Liberal Association (U.L.A.) was planning for February, which would be held in Belfast's Ulster Hall.

The proposed speakers in Belfast included the young Liberal M.P. Winston Churchill and key nationalists from the Irish Parliamentary Party such as Joe Devlin. Many U.L.A. members who had tried to stay loyal to the modern Liberal agenda, now felt that Home Rule was a bitterly divisive quasi-separatist project, rather than a sagacious devolution of parliamentary democracy within the British Empire. However, others in the local U.L.A., many of them from a Catholic background, would seem to have welcomed the 3rd Home Rule Bill and embraced it with open arms.[85]

Some Ballymena Liberals such as John Dinsmore, a rural district councillor and woollen manufacturer from Kells, thought that the best compromise might be to allow Irish Home Rule to pass but to exclude the north-east. At a meeting in Whiteside's Hotel in the town, he advocated one parliament for what he called 'Catholic Ireland' and another for the 'four or five counties of North East Ulster'. At this meeting, widely various views were expressed. Some members expressed opposition to any kind of Home Rule but some wanted to see Home Rule passed without any additional splitting of Ireland into two different political regimes.

Those members who rejected the entire Home Rule project turned out to be the majority in Ballymena, as they were in almost every other part of Ulster. During the course of January, the local newspapers reported that the Mid-Antrim Liberals had seceded from the U.L.A. John Paton, described in the press as a 'manufacturer's agent' from Linenhall Street and the secretary of the group, sent a letter to the organisers of the Ulster Hall meeting, indicating that in the view of most Ballymena members, there was 'no half-way house between Liberalism and Home Rule.' In due course, the Ulster Hall meeting had to be moved form its city centre location and reconvened within the nationalist redoubt of Catholic West Belfast due to fears of violence, after unionists in the city vowed to prevent the meeting from taking place.

For John Dinsmore this was an embittering period, during which he felt that his fellow-Liberals in Mid-Antrim had backed down from their duty to honour the cause of political reform in Ireland and from considering even some kind of pragmatic compromise position. Before long, he would speak up more vehemently and unreservedly for the Home Rule legislation. And as will be seen at a later stage in this narrative, he would make the controversial argument that 'the bigotry drum' was being beaten in Ballymena, purely in order to further the wealth of Mid-Antrim's unionist leaders, such as John Young of Galgorm Castle.

John Dinsmore would appear to have cherished a family memory of an ancestor who had been gaoled in Carrickfergus Castle as a United Irishman. His granddaughter still recalled, when interviewed in 2011, that he was a gentleman with a vast library of historical and geographical books and a love of ornithology. He possessed a number of pet Irish Wolfhounds, including a huge dog called Bran. Earlier in his career, Dinsmore

85. *Ballymena Weekly Telegraph*, 6, 13 January 1912.

had spent time at Leeds Technical College, learning more about the modern craft of woollen manufacture. Other members of his family were entirely supportive of the unionist project but John Dinsmore seems to have retained good relations not only with them but with neighbours such as the ardent unionist cleric, the Reverend O.W. Clarke of St Saviour's Church in Connor.

Going against the views of the majority of one's co-religionists was not just a Protestant phenomenon. A man who signed himself as James McMullan and indicated that he was a Catholic from Ahoghill, wrote about his opposition to the Home Rule project in local papers. He was particularly opposed to the ancient Order of Hibernians, whom he saw as a secret society with dark intentions. He wrote letters to the press, complaining that the A.O.H. often compelled Catholics to become members and that they even resorted to 'waylaying and beating' those who refused to join. McMullan also deplored the debauchery that allegedly took place on A.O.H. premises, when such shocking things as 'drinking and dancing' were quite openly permitted.[86] Given that the 1911 census reveals only one man of this name and religious affiliation in the town - and that he was a young agricultural labourer - it is hard to know what to make of this precocious outburst of censorious disapproval.[87]

The development of a local unionist leadership

Meanwhile throughout March the cause of unionism in Mid-Antrim continued to grow in strength and self-confidence. A new Unionist Club was founded in Buckna and at a ceremonial meeting in the local Orange Hall, Willy Young addressed the assembled crowd who had entered through a doorway above which a banner had been placed, which proclaimed 'One Flag, One Throne.'

Young engaged in the customary denunciations of Irish nationalists and English Liberals who were all engaged in 'nefarious machinations to try and break up the British Empire'. Conscious of the deeply Presbyterian culture and proud planter roots of the local people, he told them that it was on 'the position that Presbyterians took up in this great fight that the future of Ulster depended.' He went on to express his admiration for:

> 'that splendid race of men...with Anglo-Scottish blood' who had, he claimed, found Ireland to be 'a sterile waste' when they arrived and 'turned it into a land of fertility and plenty.'

Young also focused on what he believed to be the strong military traditions of this part of Ulster. He was greeted with warm applause when he 'reminded' them that:

> 'they sent Sir George White to the British Army...a man of their own blood and race who kept the flag flying gloriously at Ladysmith.'

Another veteran of the South African War made one of his regular appearances in the district during March. Sir Arthur O'Neill and his wife Annabel opened a new 'reading room' in Broughshane, which was situated in a building granted by the O'Neill family. In the premises there was a range of leisure facilities, including billiards tables, chess boards and boxes of dominos. A garden adjacent to the reading room was soon to be converted into a space for outdoor games. Indoors, a 'handsome clock' had been installed, having been presented to the

---

86. *Ballymena Weekly Telegraph*, 10 February 1912.

87. Census of Ireland 1911 (http://www.census.nationalarchives.ie/search/) (24 September 2010).

local people by Lady O'Neill. In the course of the evening, a short concert took place, which included a mix of Irish ballads such as *Darling girl from Clare* and imperial anthems such as *The Sea is England's glory*:

> 'Thou loveliest land of beauty
> Where dwells domestic worth,
> Where loyalty and duty
> Entwine each heart and hearth,
> Thy rock is freedom's pillow,
> The rampart of the brave!
> Oh, long as rolls the billow,
> Shall England rule the wave!'[88]

One other development in Mid-Antrim during March was the foundation of a Women's Unionist Association in response to encouragement from the headquarters of the Ulster Women's Unionist Council. At the first meeting, Lady O'Neill was elected as president and Willy Young's wife Mary Alice became vice-president, although almost all the speakers on the platform were men. John Young offered some very practical advice, telling the women who were present to 'control the men' and 'see to it that they voted the right way.' The Reverend Haslett went so far as to suggest that 'women could take some part by peaceful methods' in the unionist campaign.

And there was a growing sense in Ballymena that the anti-Home Rule campaign was becoming a grand and substantial affair. At the Women's Unionist meeting in March, a Mr Webb declared from the platform that theirs was going to be 'the biggest political movement that the United Kingdom had ever seen.' Webb's speech also revealed the strong and arguably inflated sense of their own significance that some Ballymena unionists now possessed. He declared that 'the name of Ballymena was a household word in America' and that it was clearly 'the most progressive town in Ireland' which was a prime reason why it 'ought to be in the front of the firing line' in the struggle for the preservation of the Union, which Ulster would face in the months that lay ahead.

Samuel Hood offered familiar themes for consideration, suggesting that 'Providence was guiding the cause' of Ulster 'as it did the ancient Israelites' and stressing that Ulstermen should 'resist unto the shedding of blood' if their rights as Britons were threatened. Motifs from the Old Testament scriptures and vivid remembrances of past battles had been part of loyalist iconography for a long time and they made an appearance each summer on Orange banners.[89]

Religious animosity and street politics in Ballymena

During the first few months of 1912, throughout the more peripheral or more rural areas of Mid-Antrim where Catholics were either in the majority or else made up a substantial part of the population, the passage of the 3rd Home Rule Bill was awaited with enthusiasm. One such area was Glenravel, just a few miles north-east of Ballymena, where Ireland's literary tradition was much celebrated. On 6th January, the local drama group produced the well-known Irish melodrama *The Colleen Bawn* by Dion Boucicault, to great acclaim.

---

88. Details of Young's and O'Neill's speeches are found in *Ballymena Observer*, 1, 8 March, 1912.

89. Details of the speeches at the Women's Unionist meeting are found in *Ballymena Observer*, 22 March 1912.

Image 22. Garfield Place, Ballymena, which was a cul de sac of terraced houses, built by Patrick Owens for workers in the adjacent seed mill. Local unionist politicians asked householders such as these to fly the Union flag on 'Ulster Day', 28 September 1912, during the signing of the Ulster Covenant. (Mid-Antrim Museum collection)

In areas such as Portglenone, to the west of Ballymena, where Irish music and dance were greatly favoured, members of a local dance class staged one of their popular presentations in the latter part of January during which a series of jigs and reels was performed by the dancers. Several patriotic poems were recited and a song about the 1798 Rising was rendered by a local singer. The audience heard how the song was of special contemporary significance, given that it had been written by the daughter of John Redmond.

In the vicinity of Crebilly to the east of Ballymena, which had a significant Catholic population, the ongoing plight of the less prosperous parts of the Irish countryside in an era of sustained emigration had motivated local women to form a branch of the 'Union of United Irishwomen' during January. The United Irishwomen had been formed in 1911 and were affiliated to the Irish Agricultural Association, whose stated aim was to promote the wellbeing of rural communities, by drawing in country-women to the task of improving the quality of daily life, 'irrespective of creed or class.'[90]

The pain of mass-emigration was felt much more acutely in hilly and less fertile country areas than in the substantial town of Ballymena, which had grown in size, despite Ireland's overall population decline in the decades after the Famine. During January, a play on the topic of local emigration was written and performed in Cushendall reading room by a committee of Glens inhabitants who were deeply concerned that the unique rural culture of their relatively remote upland and coastal area was under threat as young men and women left for America, to get away from an existence that for all its cultural riches and natural beauty, offered too little

---

90. Details of events in Crebilly, Portglenone and Glenravel are found in *Ballymena Weekly Telegraph*, 6, 13, 20, 27 January 1912.

by way of gainful employment and opportunity.[91]

Of course, many Glens folk had made their way to Ballymena in search of employment in recent decades and they now formed a substantial part of the Catholic population of the town. In March 1912, most of these Ballymena Catholics would have experienced a tense time, as a contentious law-suit made its way through the courts and stirred up 'party feeling' in its wake.

The dispute had it origins in the first few months of 1911. John Wilson, who had been a servant of Reverend Gilmour, the minister of the Wellington Street Presbyterian church, was involved in a road accident involving a vehicle owned by the local council. He then sought legal compensation. Gilmour expected that Wilson would approach James Clarke to take on his case. Clarke was church secretary at Wellington Street and a busy lawyer. Instead, to Gilmour's distress, Wilson approached John McCann, a young Catholic lawyer with nationalist sympathies who was prominent in the cultural life of the town. What offended Gilmour about this choice was that during recent public disputes over the *Ne Temere* decree, it was McCann's brother who had fled from his Protestant wife, declaring that their marriage in a Protestant church, conducted by Reverend Gilmour, was null and void. Gilmour had then become a sustained and outspoken critic of McCann's behaviour and the Catholic teaching which had apparently motivated it.

In letters penned during July and August 1911, Reverend Gilmour had told Wilson:

> 'everyone is surprised that you, an Orangeman, would be running after the Romanists and employing McCann.'

He also suggested that if Wilson abandoned McCann in favour of Clarke, then there would be a much greater chance of success, as Clarke would be able to assemble evidence that McCann did not have the ability to access. When John McCann was shown this letter by his client, the young lawyer reckoned that Gilmour had brought him into disrepute and so he decided to have the cleric charged with libel, seeking £2,000 damages. By the last week in February 1912, the case had come up for hearing in Dublin.

During the course of the trial, the Ballymena clergyman was subjected to incisive questioning by a barrister who suggested that his behaviour was shameful and highly un-Christian, particularly given that Gilmour was a 'servant of God.' Suggestions were made that personal animus had led the Ballymena clergyman to portray McCann in a bad light. However, McCann's lawyer was unable to prove that Gilmour's letter had been libellous and so at the conclusion of the court proceedings the cleric was deemed not guilty of the charge.

However, the story of the trial was carried in detail on the pages of the northern newspapers and stirred up great anger in Ballymena. The intensive and at times abrasive questioning which one of their respected senior clergymen had undergone would appear to have caused much resentment in the town. The inquisition which Gilmour had endured seemed perhaps to point towards the hostility which Protestant clerics might face in the 'new dispensation,' under the much-dreaded rule of a 'Catholic-dominated' parliament.

On the night that the trial of Gilmour concluded, trouble began to brew in Ballymena. *Telegraph* recorded how unrest had started as 'drumming parties made a detour of the principal streets of the town and a procession was formed, in front of which an effigy of the plaintiff in the case was carried'. The paper went on

---

91. *Ballymena Observer*, 12 January 1912.

to describe how 'windows in the houses of several of the local inhabitants were damaged by stone-throwing, several of them being smashed.' Later, on a 'waste plot' on the Galgorm Road, an effigy of McCann was burned. The procession then cheered and sang and marched back into town. The police, who attended the scene, were intent on preventing serious damage to the property of several 'supposed sympathisers' of McCann's.

Image 23. The Ballymena lawyer and prominent Catholic, John Patrick McCann, who instigated a libel case against Reverend Gilmour of Wellington Street Presbyterian Church. Subsequently, angry crowds burnt McCann's effigy on the Galgorm Road. (Photograph donated by the McCann family)

The newspaper article concluded with the comment that there was now 'much regret all round' about the evening's events. However, this was not the end of the matter. A few days later, approximately forty people were brought before the town court accused of 'indecent behaviour.' On the night of the demonstration, Head Constable Masterson of Harryville Barracks had confronted one particular man who was burning McCann's effigy. That man had then taken up a 'fighting attitude.' He called Masterson a number of unpleasant names and threatened to 'knock the face' off him, for which the R.I.C. man had summonsed him.

Masterson indicated that the accused persons who now stood in court had been in a crowd of several hundred which had engaged in obstreperous behaviour, walking past a house belonging to the McCann family singing 'party songs' before they moved on to stand outside 'Mr Quinn's public house.' According to Masterson, several girls had been particularly vocal and a number of these young women were amongst the group which had been summonsed and who now stood in court.

The magistrate then heard from Masterson how the crowd, which was allegedly 500 strong, walked to a public house belonging to the McCann family on the Waveney Road, breaking windows in property belonging to the McConnell family on the way. Outside the pub, the crowd grew very noisy indeed and one of the McCanns, at some considerable risk, came out and tried to reason with them. It was to no avail as stones were then thrown at his windows.

Masterson then indicated that this crowd of 'mill girls and boys' had seen a well-known local 'home ruler' making his way along the street in a pony and trap and had surrounded him, giving him a considerable fright although no physical harm was done. Masterson expressed his disappointment regarding one particular young man who now stood accused of intimidating behaviour and who worked as a cleaner in the Harryville barracks.

Defending the accused in court was James Clarke. He was accompanied by another lawyer, John Adrain. The two lawyers indicated that like many people in Ballymena they were incensed that the Royal Irish Constabulary had summonsed so many young men and women. Clarke made it clear that the crowd had gathered to register a legitimate protest against the treatment of Reverend Gilmour and that that crowd had included 'merchants, solicitors, clergymen and people of all denominations.' Clarke suggested that large and emotional crowds had often gathered in Ballymena during times of high drama, as when news broke of the relief of Ladysmith, during the Boer War.

But on this occasion, the crowd had unfortunately included a few 'irresponsible youths' and 'smaller fry' who had thrown stones, although the people standing in court had had nothing to do with this. Clarke and Adrain argued that it was quite reprehensible that a few 'poor people' should have been dragged into court, and have their names sullied in this way, facing a possible fine which they could ill afford to pay. They had 'a perfect right to do all that was done,' the two lawyers claimed.

They went on to argue that Masterson had a 'grudge' against 'the fellows from the foundry,' at which someone in the court shouted out 'Clabber Street!' The two lawyers also stated that in calling for extra police to be brought into the town on the night of the demonstration, Masterson had over-reacted and damaged the good name and peaceable reputation of Ballymena, which was an issue that had led Sir Arthur O'Neill to ask questions about police over-reaction in the House of Commons. The two lawyers went on to argue that the crowd had been under severe provocation from 'vagabonds' who had had 'the audacity to sing, on the streets of Ballymena' the well-known rebel ballad *The Boys of Wexford*, which celebrated the exploits of the United Irishmen at the battle of Vinegar Hill in 1798:

'We are the boys of Wexford
Who fought with heart and hand
To burst in twain the galling chain
And free our native land...

...and if for want of leaders
We lost at Vinegar Hill
We're ready for another fight
And love our country still...'

Clarke praised the 'restraint' of the people who came on to the streets during the protest against John McCann, saying that 'it speaks well for the crowd that they did not make an attack on these vagabonds.'

In an emotional climax to their defence of the accused, Clarke and Adrain stated that the behaviour of the police in summonsing so many local people simply could 'not be tolerated'. The two lawyers declared that the summonses were 'a disgrace to the town and a disgrace to the urban council' who should have advised the R.I.C. not to go ahead with the court proceedings. Turning to Head Constable Masterson, Clarke said 'it is this man that is the cause of the whole trouble' and he accused him of regularly 'sneaking' and 'skulking' about in order to snare people and then 'pouncing out' to issue undeserved summonses.

The Justice of the Peace, a Mr Holmes, seemed convinced by the argument proposed by Clarke and Adrain and decided to dismiss the case against the group of men and women that Masterson had summonsed. However, given his awareness that trouble might be brewing tonight on the streets of the town, he decided that that dismissal would come only after another hearing in a few weeks' time. This proposal was seized on angrily by the two lawyers who wished for a complete and immediate clearance of the charges, a plea which was not granted however. Then as the resident magistrate brought events to a close, the large crowd which had gathered in the courthouse gave a loud cheer and before they left the building they sang a vigorous rendition of the National Anthem.

That night, there was indeed another demonstration in Ballymena and an effigy of Masterson in a R.I.C. uniform was carried through the town in a 'handcart,' accompanied by a 'drumming party'. The effigy was then burned on the Galgorm Road. *Telegraph* reported that a crowd of 'several thousands' was walking the streets and that several speeches had been made in the course of the evening, requesting good order and advising against 'stone-throwing'. At one stage, so as to indicate that the police in general were not the target of the community's anger, there were requests for 'cheers' for District Inspector Ross. There were also cheers for the defending solicitors. According to *Telegraph*, the crowd then departed in an orderly manner.[92]

In due course, the cases against those who had been accused by the police of 'indecent behaviour' were dismissed. Somewhat tired perhaps by the events of the past few weeks, Reverend Gilmour was glad to achieve special recognition during April for his twenty-five years of service as the minister of Wellington Street. At the anniversary celebration he was praised as an exemplary servant of God and as a man who was 'worthy of the Great Master'. Gilmour was presented with a 'purse of sovereigns' and given space and time to enjoy 'a well-deserved holiday.'

Playing a key part in the evening's proceedings was the church secretary, James Clarke. In a recent ceremony at the Protestant Hall, he had been presented with a clock and some attractive ornaments by the girls he had defended for their participation in public protests against John McCann. During the course of the evening, Councillor George Hanna indicated his belief that the McCann case had been part of a nationalist plot to belittle Ballymena and to bring it down to 'the level of towns in the south and west' of Ireland. This argument was endorsed by Reverend Gilmour, who suggested that the whole sorry episode must be connected with recent 'attempts being made...to discredit the north...' and in particular to sully the 'fair name of the town.'

James Clarke responded to the other speakers by praising the virtues of Ballymena in which he had been 'born and bred', saying that there was 'no town like it.' Once again, he defended the actions of the young women who had taken to the streets to defend the honour of Reverend Gilmour, stating that he 'hoped that his children would look on the action of the young girls with pleasure.'

92. For details of the libel trial in Dublin, the civic disturbances and the subsequent legal proceedings in Ballymena's town hall, see *Ballymena Weekly Telegraph* 2, 9, 16 March 1912.

He also congratulated the magistrates on having come to a sensible conclusion with regard to the case and he thanked the press for their fair, detailed coverage of the whole painful episode.[93] However, the memory of this frightening period undoubtedly lived on in the minds of those people whose homes had been attacked and in the wider nationalist community. And when a particularly controversial public political statement was made by another Ballymena clergyman in the weeks that lay ahead, it provoked a response from a prominent County Antrim Catholic who was far enough removed from the town to feel safe enough to register his concerns.

Political combat in the local press

A public speech by Reverend F.D. Simpson was quoted in *Ballymena Observer* in May 1912, in which he had referred to Irish Home Rule as an opportunity for 'Rome' to exert 'the rule of a foreign power in our free country.' This was a typical public utterance in Ulster at this time, as was his statement that 'Protestant home rulers' merely sought advancement within a future Home Rule regime and were a collection of pathetic 'place-hunters...guided only by self-interest and worldly principle.'

However, Simpson had then suggested, more controversially, that Irish Catholics, whilst they were invariably a 'kind' and 'neighbourly' people, were quite 'unfitted to be wise, impartial rulers of any land' because of their religious allegiances. This was a comment which carried the stark implication that Catholics were endemically incapable of self-government.

Joseph O'Kane J.P. from Ballycastle responded to Simpson's missive. He said he was deeply disturbed by the way a Presbyterian cleric could so 'wantonly insult his Catholic fellow countrymen' and he expressed dismay that Simpson should imply that the 'full civil liberty' of being able to stand as a politician or a public leader 'cannot be conceded to Catholics, anywhere, at any time.' He wondered if it was attitudes like Simpson's that had caused 'respectable inhabitants of Ballymena to be burnt in effigy recently and the windows of those who do not see eye to eye with Mr Simpson to be broken.'

The writer went on to question the unionist claim that nationalists always submitted political projects to the leadership of priests. He suggested that the kind of Protestant clergyman currently found in Ballymena was 'a sort of despot' who was prepared to 'occupy a political platform' and to tell all Protestants what they should think. O'Kane also noted that freedom of religion existed in several European countries where the majority of the population was Catholic and he drew attention to the 'intolerant' nature of the Westminster Confession of Faith. This was a 17th century theological document to which the Presbyterian denomination adhered and O'Kane proposed that it was a savage treatise which condemned all 'infidels, papists' and 'other idolators' to eternal punishment. O'Kane also doubted whether Christ would have wished to see his kingdom divided into 'a hundred warring sects' which seemed to be the result of the Protestant rejection of a central papal authority. Correspondence between O'Kane and Simpson took place in *Observer* over a period of several weeks, during which the Ballycastle man offered his hope that Protestants would 'decline to shiver any longer on the banks of the Boyne, or mutter the old shibboleths of dissension'.

He also extended an invitation to Protestants to join their fellow-countrymen in journeying towards the future.[94] Such an invitation invariably had no appeal for the unionists of Ballymena if it involved journeying away from the Union but if it meant living alongside Catholics and agreeing to differ on matters of belief

---

93. The presentation evenings for Reverend Gilmour and for James Clarke are both described in *Ballymena Weekly Telegraph*, 27 April 1912.

94. The religious and political arguments between Simpson and O'Kane continued each week in *Ballymena Observer*, 24 May - 28 June 1912.

whilst the town continued to make good commercial progress, then they were usually quite happy with the idea. No further major outbreaks of trouble took place in Mid-Antrim. Before long, John McCann and James Clarke were re-engaged in conflict, but only on everyday legal issues within the constrained arena of the local courts.

However, it is clear that all through the spring of 1912, local unionist leaders were in no way disposed to tone down their rhetoric. Towards the end of March, as Cullybackey loyalists gathered to make arrangements for the grand Easter Tuesday demonstration, they were addressed by Mr Haughton, owner of the mill where many of them worked. He encouraged them to remember their heritage and be proud of the economic success which this part of Ulster had achieved. Voicing the not uncommon Protestant perception of Irish nationalists as prone to idleness and fecklessness, he pleaded with his hearers not to 'give up what they had laboured for to a lot of loafers and corner boys'. He also asked his audience to remember that most nationalists were 'ruled by the church of Rome and the Pope' and that if nationalism succeeded then Protestants would be made to yield to 'priest-craft and Roman Catholicism.'[95]

Mid-Antrim politics during the spring and summer of 1912

During Easter an anti-Home Rule gathering took place at Balmoral in Belfast. A contingent from the Mid-Antrim Unionist Clubs, which had been practising their marching for several weeks, took part in the grand parade which processed through the agricultural show-grounds. The local groups were led by Sir Arthur O'Neill and 'their soldierly appearance was favourably commented on' on the pages of *Observer*. The newspaper proclaimed that the unionists who were parading at Balmoral were now 'a citizen army, marching with astonishing military precision...to the patriotic airs of countless bands of fifers.'[96]

Shortly afterwards, when speaking at a ceremony for the unveiling of a new banner for local members of the Royal Black Institution, George Young mentioned the 'quiet drilling that had been going on in the Orange lodges for months and the marches out on the roads', all of which had borne fruit at Balmoral.[97] As spring turned into summer, more daylight hours were available and the sight of a group of men marching in military formation down the country roads of County Antrim became a familiar sight although at this stage there was little sign of uniforms and only an infrequent display of guns. In the newspapers, stirring loyalist poetry became a regular feature:

> 'We are the guardians of that creed
> Which giveth all and does not barter
> But sows in breasts its living seed
> And bids its gallant servants bleed
> Or die, to keep the Lord's own charter!
> Ulster, if broken, will not bend,
> It goes to our appointed end.'[98]

---

95. *Ballymena Observer*, 29 March 1912.

96. *Ballymena Observer*, 12 April 1912.

97. *Ballymena Observer*, 10 May 1912.

98. *Ballymena Weekly Telegraph*, 11 May 1912.

And speakers at various loyalist rallies often broke out into highly emotive verse, as when Mrs Mercier Clements addressed the Mid-Antrim Unionist Women's Association in May:

> 'Tis the voice of Ulster calling
> With her heart both loud and high,
> And ere she forfeits freedom
> She must know the reason why
> And if her friends forsake her
> And their faith be almost fled,
> Then the bloody hand of Ulster
> Will be dyed a deeper red.'[99]

If the unionist leaders of Mid-Antrim were now troubled that Britain might abandon them to their Home Rule fate, they set out with renewed energy to proclaim their devotion to the mother country on Empire Day, 24th May 1912. At Galgorm, the Young family once again provided food and drink for the locals and flags and bunting were erected throughout the village. The Reverend E.D. Sweetman, 'attired in Boy Scouts uniform,' addressed the crowd and explained the way in which an empire worked, which he felt was not dissimilar to the operation of the mill where so many of them were employed. The important parallel was that everyone worked together for the greater common good.

Image 24. Boy Scouts with their scoutmaster, outside Galgorm National School, complete with drill sticks. Scouting had been founded in 1907 and quickly spread across the Empire. Young Protestants in Ballymena and its hinterland were encouraged to join the scouts as they were elsewhere in Ulster, participating in ceremonial and imperial occasions such as the funeral of Sir George White V.C. (Young collection, Mid-Antrim Museum)

---

99. *Ballymena Observer*, 24 May 1912.

Sweetman then claimed that the British Empire was 'made by Boy Scouts...' who were invariably 'gentle and courteous and fit to rule men.' He noted that Scouts always obeyed orders and he pointed the local boys to the exemplary, if doomed, courage shown in the Crimean War by the soldiers in the Light Brigade, of whom the poet Lord Tennyson had once said 'Theirs but to do or die.'[100]

Meanwhile, the cultural life of those Irishmen and women who were more interested in Irish than British history continued in County Antrim. An inspiring annual ceremony at the Shane O'Neill commemorative cairn took place in early summer, within the seemingly untainted, pre-plantation landscape of the Glens, on a hill-top overlooking the vast expanses of the Irish Sea. The cairn had been recently erected by Francis Joseph Bigger in an attempt to rekindle the memory of the epic 16th century struggle of the Gaelic clans against English dominance.

The Glens Feis took place later in the summer and several children from Harryville took part in an 'under eight Irish speaking' competition, while a number of older children from other parts of Ballymena participated in the senior contest. The judges noted that the Ballymena entrants were less experienced than children from other areas but felt encouraged by their efforts and recommended that they practise more. At the Feis there were prizes for essays on three different topics. One subject was the great Irish saint, Columba. Another topic dealt with the numerous soldiers known loosely as the 'Irish Brigade', who - as exiled Irishmen - had fought with continental armies in bygone years. The third subject was the eighteenth century Irish patriot and politician, Henry Grattan.[101]

Events at the recent Feis were of little interest to most of the mourners at the funeral of Sir George White, the military hero who was buried in Broughshane in early July, his body having been brought back from Belfast to Ballymena by train where George Young was waiting with a company of the Galgorm Scouts. The funeral cortege made its way slowly through the streets between lines of solemn onlookers who no doubt felt that they were participating in a grand imperial ceremony. However, among the mourners was Sir George's son Jack, who by 1912 had left behind his military career with a Scottish regiment for a life of experimental modernity. He had married a Gibralterian girl, embraced vegetarianism then returned to a carnivorous existence while attempting to run a chicken farm. He had read various German philosophers, embraced mysticism, existed as a 'tramp' for a while, and in recent months had been living in an anarchist colony in the Cotswolds in the south-west of England. He was opposed to the political rivalries that were threatening to tear Ireland apart and he was becoming more and more convinced that:

> 'the warring creeds and races in Ireland had to be fused...by some catalytic agent that had not yet emerged.'

By the summer of his father's funeral, Jack White was becoming convinced that socialism was the very catalyst that the working class needed in order to unite, to mobilise and to effect a revolution that would move Irish society beyond bitter, long-standing internal conflict.[102] There were few signs that Ballymena's working class had the stomach for that level of class-war, even though another industrial dispute did break out in the town

---

100. *Ballymena Observer*, 31 May 1912.

101. *Ballymena Observer*, 28 June 1912 and *Ballymena Weekly Telegraph*, 15, 29 June, 1912.

102. White's early career is described in his republished biography - Jack White, *Misfit* (Dublin, 2005) See p 101 for the quotation mentioned here.

during July when workers at Kane's foundry went on strike over the familiar issue of long and unsocial working hours.[103]

White might of course have suggested, within the terms of a revolutionary socialist analysis, that the 'works outing' to the seaside which John Young facilitated each summer was an insurance strategy to maintain the ongoing loyalty of his employees! In 1912 the excursion headed to Larne by the light railway which connected the two towns. A day's wages were granted despite absence from the workplace and cheap rail tickets were readily available with some young employees even qualifying for free tickets and some pocket money. At Larne Town Hall, music was laid on and there was an opportunity for a dance, before the workers retuned to the railway station for the journey home.[104]

The Castledawson Sunday School outrage and its aftermath

But the painful religious conflict that Jack White so abhorred had already come into view during the summer, when a group of adults, children and teachers, who were on a Sunday School outing to Castledawson, came into confrontation with nationalists belonging to the Ancient Order of Hibernians. They had seen the Union flags which the group from Belfast were carrying - it was not uncommon for Protestant Sunday School excursions to carry Union flags during this era. The Hibernians had been 'on parade' and they were accompanied by men who carried ceremonial pikes, which had been the Irish weapons of war during the 1798 Rebellion. Some of the Hibernians had - allegedly - proceeded to throw stones at the party and a full riot soon developed, involving local loyalists as well as local nationalists. There was an attempt at riot control with fixed bayonets by men of the Royal Irish Constabulary, which eventually succeeded in bringing the violence to a stop.

The incident was guaranteed to cause particular fury due to the stark symbolism of the pikes and the harm caused to a number of small children. However, public debate in Ulster ensued, focusing on whether provocation had been offered to nationalists by members of a flute band which accompanied the Sunday School party on its journey from Belfast and by local loyalists who had taken the opportunity to swell the ranks of the procession.[105]

As the news of the incident came through, scores of Catholic workers were attacked and expelled from the Belfast shipyards. Some of these men ended up in hospital, where they had to be treated for severe injuries. Senior Protestant clergy such as the Presbyterian Moderator (or leader), Henry Montgomery, called for 'forbearance and restraint.' But even in the smaller, quieter County Antrim town of Carrickfergus, there were attacks on Catholic property. In the nationalist press, there were accusations that the Castledawson incident had been portrayed by unionists as much more vicious than it actually was, and that it had become an excuse for the much more widespread ill-treatment of innocent Catholics. *Irish News* lamented a situation where 'the people' were 'fighting one another like rabid dogs.' And it accused unionism of playing an inflammatory role in Irish politics.[106]

---

103. *Ballymena Observer*, 26 July 1912.

104. *Ballymena Observer*, 23 August 1912.

105. The Castledawson incident and its aftermath was covered in the two local papers throughout late July and early August. It was covered in a range of other Irish newspapers - see in particular *Belfast Telegraph* and *Irish News*, 1-6 July 1912.

106. See *Ballymena Weekly Telegraph*, 20 July 1912, for news of the Carrickfergus attacks. Varying coverage of the shipyard expulsions and tension on the streets of the city may be found in *Irish News* and *Belfast News Letter* throughout July and August 1912, in particular during 1-6 July.

Image 25. St Patrick's Church Of Ireland in Castle Street, whose minister, Canon Ross, counselled caution during the tense and difficult days of the Home Rule Crisis. (Mid-Antrim Museum collection)

No reprisals were reported in the newspapers in Mid-Antrim, although the attack on the Sunday School group had taken place just 16 miles from Ballymena. However, the Hibernians of Castledawson featured as figures of contempt and disgust in many speeches delivered during the 1912 parading season along with the usual villains such as 'Protestant home rulers,' the mention of whom often drew a loud 'boo' from a loyalist crowd.

Speaking at a rally near Kells, Sir Arthur O'Neill welcomed the fact that because of the marching and drilling regularly undertaken by the Unionist Clubs, men were becoming 'physically fit and well-disciplined...' He believed that they were also learning the self-restraint that military training engenders. He stressed the horror of the Castledawson incident but he also expressed regret for the expulsions from the shipyards and said that Orangemen must show self-discipline rather than engaging in random retaliation. It was left to another speaker at the demonstration to touch more vividly on the sense of outrage that many local Protestants felt about the way in which 'defenceless children and women' had been 'stabbed with pikes and beaten by sticks.' Referring scathingly to the British Prime Minister's recent call for Ulster's unionists to show a more courteous attitude, the speaker declared that 'the victim in sight of the stake...had little time for courtesy.' Stories of Protestants being burned at the stake were to be found in iconic texts such as *Foxe's Book of Martyrs*.

As well as covering events at Kells, *Observer* also dealt with demonstrations at Ahoghill and Portglenone where the Reverend W.H. Lee gave expression to his deepest fears. For him, the 'Castledawson outrage' offered grim evidence that the Irish Parliamentary Party and their Hibernian fellow-travellers were a 'mob of would-be child murderers' and a bunch of 'papist rebels' who had been nurtured by the 'blood-stained, crime-saturated, so-called Church of Rome.' He called on the Protestant men of Ulster to form themselves into a fully-fledged army. That meant not just 'smashing a few panes of glass or storming the police' but 'real warfare, waged with the grim determination of men who were fighting for their life, their liberty and their faith.' His call was met with resounding cheers from the listening crowd.

Lee continued to tell them that 'the day for platform platitudes' was past and 'the time for action had arrived'. It was time to find money to 'procure the necessary arms and equipment' to teach nationalists a lesson. These nationalists would find that 'they were up against something bigger than a Sunday School excursion'. And as far as the Liberal government was concerned, the only argument that these Englishmen would listen to was 'the whistle of the bullet and the shriek of the shell.' Lee then focused on arming the Unionist Clubs. He asked why rifle clubs were not forming in the neighbourhood and suggested that Protestants needed to practise on their own rifle butts, in order to wage 'grim and real warfare'. The Ahoghill cleric was clearly aware that a number of Unionist Club members across Ulster had formed rifle clubs by this time, facilitating practice in the use of firearms.[107]

The M.P. William Carson focused on the economic side of the Anti-Home Rule argument and stressed that under a Dublin government northern businesses would be 'taxed off the face of the earth' and would have to 'bid farewell to all capital and labour, goodbye to all thrift and industry' and the country would be 'overrun by hordes of idle, lazy vagabonds.'[108]

The Reverend Lee returned to his emotive theme, when speaking in mid-August at an Apprentice Boys' service in Ballymena. Once more he condemned 'the corrupt communion of the church of Rome' and recommended that listeners purchase a history of the Protestant Reformation and read about the 'awful savagery and butchery and hypocrisy' of the Catholic Church. He argued that the Ancient Order of Hibernians was part of that grim tradition, and that it was prepared to 'walk knee deep, if necessary, in Protestant blood.' Indeed, it might re-employ the 'stake and rack' of the Spanish Inquisition.

Lee assured them that as a 'south of Ireland man' he had witnessed things that would 'make their blood boil'. He concluded by urging his audience to stand up for truth and heed the call of Christ, which - apparently - included the divine injunction to 'wear my colours' and 'work and fight under my glorious banner.'[109]

Even in the wake of positive events such as the Ballymena Home Industries Associations' festival in September, religious and political fears continued to be intense. The festival had involved a fine array of items, such as crochet work, bedspreads, Irish lace, and displays of local baking and wood carving. But the vulnerability of this prosperous Mid-Antrim array was seemingly on the mind of a platform speaker at the formation of the Ahoghill Unionist Club who claimed that:

'Hearths, homes and industries' would be 'trampled underfoot by the priesthood of Rome' if Home Rule eventually arrived.[110]

---

107. Evidence for these rifle clubs throughout unionist Ulster is found in Bowman, *Carson's Army*, pp 5, 21, 22.

108. Details of the speeches by O'Neill, Lee and others may be found in *Ballymena Observer*, 19 July 1912.

109. *Ballymena Observer*, 16 August 1912.

110. *Ballymena Observer*, 13 September 1912.

And on the streets, a background noise of political and religious clamour could be heard throughout the summer and early autumn of 1912, if the cases heard at the local petty sessions are to be taken as evidence. On the Monday after the 12th July celebrations, a heavily intoxicated man had been engaging in the custom of 'waking the arch'. This involved having a few alcoholic beverages on the night that the local Orange Arch was taken down, marking the end of the 'Twelfth' parades. The man was scarcely a dignified sight, walking around without his trousers on. However a violent scuffle had then broken out with an 'opposing party' and the police had been called.

Fortunately for this man, who had been summonsed by the R.I.C., James Clarke was the defending lawyer. Clarke expressed surprise that 'an opposing party had the 'cheek' to go 'where these Orangemen had a spree.' Clarke recommended that the man be 'let off' with a 'shilling fine' and in parting, the lawyer suggested darkly that such Loyalist 'sprees' would be few and far between if the Home Rule Bill was passed 'If we are to believe what we hear, this to be the last Twelfth we are going to have...'

During the summer, Clarke also defended a character who had allegedly done violence to an elderly man who, under the influence of drink, had been found 'standing up at the arch in William Street, cursing King William and shouting for Home Rule.'

James Clarke and John McCann also had an adversarial legal involvement in a case which was heard later in the year, involving two women from Alexander Street who had been found fighting each other. This tussle had involved hair-pulling, 'punches to the face' and the use of a pair of tongs and a shepherd's crook as improvised weapons. McCann argued that such disputes invariably originated in political and religious arguments conducted within the Braid Water Mill and he complained that 'when it begins in the mill they have to finish it up in Clabber Street.'

However, religious and political affiliations were not the only reason for breaches of the peace. One night in early August, a local woman with a reputation for drunken misbehaviour had engaged in 'refractory conduct' in the grounds of the workhouse, smashing thirteen panes of glass, after scaling the wall on finding that the gates were locked on her late return from a 'night on the town'. A report on her vandalism in a local paper suggested that she was, perhaps, emulating the tactics of the suffragettes! Later in the month the minister of the Congregational Church wrote to the local papers, complaining about the fact that the windows of his church building had been smashed by stones and bottles on two successive Sunday nights. The culprits had not been caught.[111]

---

111. Details of the various cases being heard at the town hall - including those mentioned above - may be found in *Ballymena Weekly Telegraph*, 3 August - 5 October 1912.

Image 26. The People's Park in Ballymena, with drinking fountain and nearby lake. A booth was erected here for those who wished to sign the Covenant on Ulster Day. Male citizens, aged 16 and over, were able to sign in a range of venues across the town. Women could sign a separate document. (Mid-Antrim Museum collection)

Signing the Ulster Covenant in Ballymena

By early September plans were afoot for Ulster Day on the 28th of the month. This vast event would take place all across the north of Ireland and it would involve the signing of a document which had been designed to unite the unionist people in common purpose. A few months previously their leaders had pondered the idea of a pledge which everyone in the camp could sign. A suggestion was made that the 17th century Scottish Covenant was an admirable model. It was a document which had committed the Scottish Presbyterians of that era to a defence of their own distinctive form of church government, unsullied by the undue interference of bishops or an English monarch. However when the original document was consulted, it seemed linguistically and conceptually ponderous. Then under the leadership of the senior Belfast unionist Thomas Sinclair, a short, sonorous, carefully focused document known as 'Ulster's Solemn League and Covenant' was drawn up.

'Being convinced in our consciences that Home Rule would be disastrous to the material well-being of Ulster as well as of the whole island, subversive of our civil and religious freedom, destructive of our citizenship and perilous to the unity of the empire, we whose names are underwritten, men of Ulster, loyal subjects of His Gracious Majesty George V, humbly relying on the God whom our fathers in days of stress and trial confidently trusted, do hereby pledge ourselves in solemn Covenant, throughout this our time of threatened calamity, to stand by one another in defending for ourselves and for our children, our cherished position of equal citizenship in the United Kingdom, and in using all means which may be found necessary to defeat the present conspiracy to set up a Home Rule Parliament in Ireland. And in the event of such a parliament being forced upon us, we further solemnly and mutually pledge ourselves to refuse to recognise its authority. In sure confidence that God will defend the right, we hereto subscribe our names, and further we individually declare that we have not already signed this Covenant.'[112]

Although the largest mass-signing of the 'Ulster Covenant' was planned for Belfast, the unionists of Ballymena aimed to organise a similar event, as did leaders in other Ulster towns. By the first week of September George Young had made a representation to the Urban Council, asking for a change in the customary market day, so that traders would not be inconvenienced. He requested that employers permit their employees to leave their place of work in order to sign the document or preferably that traders might decide to close for the day. There was much discussion about the problems posed through loss of trade and there was a reminder from a Catholic councillor that 'Ulster Day is for some only.' A motion was passed, in which the council recommended that businesses should close on 28th September, although this would appear to have been further amended at a later stage. The motion ended up as a request that closure should occur during the afternoon, when religious services were in progress.

Throughout the month of September preparations got under way and Ballymena unionists were heartened by the brief return visit of Sir Edward Carson, who stopped off at the railway station on the 16th of the month and was greeted by a guard of honour drawn up by George Young before making a short political speech and heading on his way. At various venues, plans were drawn up for the 'big day'. Galgorm unionists had already prepared themselves, deciding at a recent meeting in the local Orange Hall to open the schoolhouse on Ulster Day for the villagers to come in and sign the document.

In Ballymena, plans soon emerged for making the Covenant available in the Protestant Hall as well as the Town Hall, the Y.M.C.A. building, the Church of Ireland's Parochial Hall, a tent in the People's Park, Harryville Mission Hall and on tables at several street corners. Any male over the age of 16 was eligible to add his name. A similar document, known as the 'Declaration', was available for women to sign. Church services were arranged for the early afternoon by the major Protestant denominations. Then at 4pm there was to be a 'demonstration' in the People's Park. Refreshments would be available at 'popular prices'.

In advance of the day, the *Observer* carried a notice directed firstly at businessmen in the town but also generally at the local population:

'The Urban District Council respectfully request that as many as possible of the merchants and traders close their business premises during the hours of divine service...and they hope that every householder will display a Union Jack...'

On the previous Monday, as excitement began to build, a unionist meeting was held in a packed Protestant Hall. Outside, several hundred people who could not gain admittance gathered in an expectant crowd. A reporter for the *Observer* noted that the speakers were accompanied from the train station to the hall by several men who carried large flaming torches. At the head of the procession the 'White's Conquerors Band' played stirring music. At the entrance to the hall a guard of honour waited, carrying swords that they proceeded to hold high over the speakers' heads like an 'arch of steel'.

When the speeches began, the crowd heard a familiar range of criticisms of the current Liberal government whom Sir Arthur O'Neill described forcefully as 'rotten' and 'depraved.' There was further criticism of the Irish

112. Details of the genesis of the Covenant document are to be found in St John Ervine, *Craigavon: Ulsterman* (London, 1949), p 103.

Image 27. The Pentagon, Ballymena. Busy junctions such as this were often crowded during Ulster Day and other unionist rallies, as people flocked to church services or came into town to see the Ulster Volunteer Force on parade. (Mid-Antrim Museum collection)

nationalist project when O'Neill's fellow M.P., J.H. Campbell, claimed that Home Rule politics was rooted in a long tradition of agrarian crime and anarchic anti-British lawlessness, including 'intimidation...moonlighting... boycotting...cattle-maiming.' The audience also heard about the detailed plans for Ulster Day and how the town would be beautifully decorated with flags, arches and 'mottoes'. They learnt of the various successes of the unionist campaign across the Irish sea where the English Tory party had begun to show keen support for the Ulster cause and where at least 100,000 sympathisers were expected to show up at an anti-Home Rule demonstration in Liverpool.

Ulster Day was pleasant and sunny in Mid-Antrim as thousands of local citizens walked to the nearest venue, where they could add their names to the Covenant or the Declaration. Four local bands played on the streets in Ballymena and some groups of men who had been practising their drill over the past few months marched in formation. As *Observer*'s reporter noted:

> 'The steady, swinging steps of the well-drilled members of the Unionist Clubs taking part gave the event something of a semi-military aspect.'

In various church services earnest prayers were said for deliverance from the hands of 'Ulster's enemies' and most of the sermons seem to have carried the same solemn moral warning that Ulster Day was no mere political rally. It was, *spiritually and morally*, a life and death affair. In the words of one speaker 'the interests of truth and righteousness' were 'at stake'.

By the end of a day that turned out to be peaceful across the north of Ireland, the crowds dispersed and the business of counting the signatures began. In due course it became clear that almost a quarter of a million men had put their names to the document, which constituted the majority of adult Protestant males in the province of Ulster. In terms of galvanising Protestant opinion and showing the rest of the world how well-organised and self-disciplined the Ulster unionists could be, this Solemn Oath and Covenant seemed to have been a success.

However for local nationalists, 28th September was a rather difficult day as the council's request for businesses to close doors in the afternoon and for all households to show a Union flag placed them in a terrible dilemma. If they did so, they were going against their pro-Home Rule convictions but if they failed to do so then they might be picked out as 'rebels.'

During Ulster Day and in the period immediately before it, some worrying rhetoric was delivered, including the injunction by one speaker at Galgorm on 13th September, that unionists should 'mark the men who did not sign' as they 'could not afford to have traitors in the camp.' Other speeches carried more measured messages, as when Sir Arthur O'Neill called at Harryville Unionist Club for no 'uncharitable' actions towards those who held different political views. He asked unionists to not 'let their patriotism get the better of them.' However O'Neill did warn his audience that physical conflict of some sort might well lie ahead. He hoped 'they would not have to bleed', nonetheless he believed that 'if bloodshed became necessary, they would have their part in it...'

This latter theme was amplified by James Clarke, who joined O'Neill on the platform. He opined that:

> 'if there was any fighting to be done...the men of Harryville and especially the working men, would not be behind in showing what side they were on.'

Sounding a more cautious note, Canon Ross participated in an Ulster Day service at St Patrick's Church of Ireland in which he called for freedom of conscience and a proper level of respect for those who did not sign, saying that 'no pressure should be put upon them.' There can be no question that a minority of local Protestants would have disapproved of the Covenant just as they did elsewhere in Ulster. And there can be no doubt that most Catholics in Mid-Antrim felt absolutely no affection for the document. They would have been worried, despite the Covenant's dignified political and religious discourse, about some of its statements of future intent, including the phrase in which unionists pledged themselves to use 'all means which may be found necessary' in order to thwart Home Rule.

And of course, if local Catholics did in fact feel gratitude for those benefits that came from living in the British Empire, they were rather unlikely to sign a document that was the keystone of a project in which very harsh comments about their religious faith were made so regularly on so many public platforms.[113]

---

113. Extensive coverage of the local preparations for and conduct of Ulster Day, including the details and quotations offered above, may be found in *Ballymena Observer*, 20, 27 September and 4 October 1912 and *Ballymena Weekly Telegraph*, 21, 28 September and 5, 12 October 1912.

The religious composition of Ballymena and district in the era of the Covenant

Of course, some Ballymena Protestants lived on streets where Catholics were actually in a majority. According to the 1911 census, 319 people lived in the relatively prosperous thoroughfare of Broughshane Street. 198 citizens were Catholic, including one man who was a local barber, two ladies who were Irish-speaking school-teachers, another man who was described in the census as a 'horse-trainer,' and another who was a 'car-driver.'

Other Ballymena Protestants lived on thoroughfares alongside a considerable minority of Catholics. In Alexander Street, with its cobblestones and 'clabber', its barefoot children and its old women dressed in shawls, Catholic residents included one elderly woman who was single and illiterate and had been registered on the census as born in India. Other Catholics on the street included a 36-year-old man who was described in the census as a 'musician' and one family which, not untypically for the era, consisted of a man and his wife with their seven children, ranging from a seven month old baby to a 19-year-old lad who was described as working in a linen factory as a 'comber'. Another Catholic family consisted of a labourer and his wife and their five children, including a 14-year-old boy and a 12-year-old girl who were both working 'in the mill'.

On Alexander Street, Catholic and Protestant often lived in the same house. One particular Protestant man lived in one of the street's more capacious houses, with his wife and step-daughter and his eight lodgers, seven of whom were Catholic. In another house, a widowed Protestant man lived with his lodger, a single Catholic labourer. In another house, a Catholic 'itinerant musician' lived with his Presbyterian wife who is denoted in the census as being a 'pedlar.' The census also records that the couple had had two children, both of whom had died at an early age. In another house, a Catholic man and woman and their three sons all co-existed with a 19-year-old boarder and the house-owner's Church of Ireland father.

Even in parts of Ballymena with a strong loyalist reputation, there were Catholic residents. In the electoral district which contained Harryville, the 1911 census showed numerous Catholics living alongside their Protestant neighbours. Bearing witness to this was the existence in Harryville of cultural features beloved of many Catholics, such as the Irish language class referred to earlier in this narrative, which was operating freely in a place where the men of the local Unionist Club were now marching and drilling on an almost nightly basis.

Many communities possessed a fairly homogenous Protestant make-up. In the 1911 census, only four of the 333 inhabitants of the locality known as 'Slaght' were registered as Catholic. In the heart of Cullybackey, the census recorded only 29 of the 545 residents as being Catholic. In the Craigywarren sector of the Kirkinriola Electoral District, only one of the 183 inhabitants was a Catholic and in one of the two Galgorm districts which feature in the census, only eight of the 139 residents were Catholic and all of them were employed as servants, including John Young's cook, kitchen maid, house maid and parlour maid.

So when Mid-Antrim Protestants were invited to sign the Covenant in September 1912, they possessed varied levels of intimacy with their Catholic fellow citizens. Some Protestants knew them as family members, as employees, work-mates, house-mates and more occasionally as employers, while others would have had little or no contact with Catholics on a day to day basis. One potential for Catholic-Protestant encounter in Mid-Antrim existed in the relationship between local citizens and their police force. In the Martinstown barracks, during the 1911 census, three of the four officers were Catholic. Each of these men was a farmer's son, and two were Irish-speakers. One man came from Roscommon, one from Donegal and one from Galway.[114]

---

114. Census for Ireland 1911 (http://www.census.nationalarchives.ie/search/) (24 September 2010).

The beginnings of a loyalist army

Amidst the gathering tensions of the Home Rule Crisis, R.I.C. officers such as these kept watching the Unionist Clubs as they continued to grow. The Harryville Club for instance had over 400 members by the end of September.[115] And to add to the tensions, a few Mid-Antrim loyalists were beginning to carry arms very openly, aided by the fact that there were now a number of rifle clubs in the district, whose members kept firearms ostensibly for recreational target practice or for shooting game.

This explicit bearing of arms was in keeping with the wishes of local leaders of the pro-Union movement. In November, *Telegraph* transcribed a statement by W.H. Webb, the Randalstown J.P., who had addressed a recent meeting in Ahoghill Orange Hall and proclaimed that Ulstermen 'wished to raise such a force that the government would not dare to send troops against them.' Reverend W.H. Lee contributed to the meeting in his customary, militant style, saying that if local loyalists 'wished a rifle range to practice shooting, he would place the rectory grounds at their disposal.' Then he broke into rhyme in order to warn his listeners:

> 'Thrice is he armed who has his cause just
> But four times armed who gets his blow in first.'

Lee said that he knew the Harryville Unionist Club was leading the way in accumulating weapons as on several occasions he had seen them marching along the roads of the district, looking particularly effective because some of them proudly carried rifles.[116] Before long, the Unionist Club members would find themselves banded together into a province-wide organisation, that attempted to provide a uniform, funds, strategy and a sub-group of businessmen and adventurers who were bent on procuring a large supply of ordnance from a foreign dealer. Soon the anti-Home Rule movement would possess a formidable, well-armed militia throughout Ulster. Already, a Belfast industrialist with strong evangelical and unionist convictions, called Fred Crawford, had placed advertisements in important European newspapers, seeking arms for Ulster.[117]

Meanwhile, those who had signed the Covenant could purchase a framed copy of the document for as little as a shilling from W. and G. Baird's in Belfast. They could read reports and see photographs of Ulster Day and all subsequent parades and rallies in their local newspapers.[118] Loyalist verse continued to adorn the pages of *Telegraph* and *Observer* including one poem which celebrated the Union flag:

> '...It flutters triumphant o'er oceans
> As free as the wind and the wave,
> And the bondsman with shackles unloosened,
> Neath its shadow's no longer a slave.'[119]

---

115. *Ballymena Weekly Telegraph*, 5 October 1912.

116. *Ballymena Observer*, 1, 29 November 1912.

117. For full details of the successful unionist attempt to buy and smuggle arms under the leadership of Fred Crawford, see Keith Haines, *Fred Crawford - Carson's gun-runner* (Donaghadee, 2009).

118. *Ballymena Weekly Telegraph*, 12 October 1912.

119. *Ballymena Weekly Telegraph*, 23 November 1912.

Image 28. A parade along the Galgorm Road by the Orange Order during the years of the Home Rule Crisis. Orange Halls were important venues for Unionist meetings and for Ulster Volunteer Force drill sessions. (Mid-Antrim Museum collection)

Occasionally, in newspaper reports, there were hints of verbal clashes between prominent unionist and nationalist citizens of the district. The Board of Guardians entered into a dispute about whether to propose an item of congratulation to be sent to Sir Edward Carson. A Mr. Gregg, who was a member of the Catholic Literary and Debating Society, suggested that 'we need not discuss either politics or politicians here at all', a sentiment with which the chairman of the board, Alexander Cowan, agreed. However, Joseph Skillen, the manager of the Phoenix Weaving Factory and a very keen unionist, was in favour of offering congratulations. In the end, the matter would appear to have been dropped.[120]

Christmas 1912

As Christmas approached, attention was focused on the pleasures of the season. The Harryville Presbyterian Church's 'bazaar and sale of work' was a great success, with a range of high quality 'jam roll, gingerbread, plum cake, soda bread and potato cake' submitted in the 'cake competition'. The 'Ballymena Orchestra' played a number of popular tunes during the second day of the event. During December, the local cinema showed highlights of Ulster's recent rugby game against the South African Springboks at Ravenhill and another popular film called *Pride of the Circus*.

A few days before Christmas, the Abbey Theatre players from Dublin came to town, brought by the ever-popular impresario, Payne Sneddon. Alongside a comedy by William Boyle, the actors performed *The Rising of the Moon* by Lady Gregory and *Kathleen ni Houlihan*, co-authored by W.B. Yeats and Lady Gregory. The final play of these three is set during the invasion of Ireland by French revolutionary soldiers in the course of the 1798 Rebellion. *Telegraph* reported that the plays 'required all the ability of the actors to make their

---

120. *Ballymena Weekly Telegraph*, 2 November 1912.

meaning clear'. It is not certain whether the reporter was referring to problems with the poetic diction and the delivery of the play in 'southern' accents that were somewhat unfamiliar to the northern ear, or whether this was a reference to confusion about the allegorical meaning of *Kathleen ni Houlihan*.

Perhaps unionist members in the audience would have struggled to grasp what the 'four green fields' in the play actually represented, and maybe they failed to grasp the identity of the old woman who had lost her 'four green fields' and needed young men to fight and die for her, in order to renew her youthfulness and claim those 'green fields' back. However nationalist members of the audience would have had little difficulty spotting that the fields were symbolic of Ireland's four provinces, that the old woman was a representation of a dying nation that needed political renewal and, most potently of all, that the entire drama was a persuasive call for young Irishmen to fight and if needs be die to liberate their country from Britain - with possible help from a foreign ally. If Ballymena needed a literary warning that armed separatism and personal sacrifice were still features of the Irish political psyche, then this was it.

Meanwhile the Ballymena newspapers had been carrying stories and photographs from the Balkans ever since territorial disputes broke out into open war in early October, involving the Ottoman Empire and several of the small, mainly Slavic nations of south-eastern Europe that had once belonged to the Turkish Caliphate. Initially, Russia had mobilised her armies, and prepared to defend her fellow-Slavs. By the end of 1912, the risk of Russian military involvement had subsided and the potential for this volatile part of Europe to initiate a wider conflict between the great empires of Europe was given little further consideration in the local press.[121]

---

121. For details of pre-Christmas preparations and elements of Ballymena's civic life in December, including the performance by actors from the Abbey Theatre, see both local newspapers for December 1912. Stories and photographs from the Balkans appeared in the Ballymena newspapers throughout the entire winter of 1912/13.

Chapter Three

1913 - The Year of the Volunteers

Chapter Three
1913 - The Year of the Volunteers

The Ulster Volunteer Force is officially formed

In January 1913, a number of unionist leaders began bringing Ulster's Unionist Club members together under the 'umbrella' of the newly formed Ulster Volunteer Force. With a central headquarters in Belfast, the U.V.F. was manned by senior military veterans from the pro-union camp and it was modelled - though only to some degree - on the structure of the British Army. It was composed of county divisions, sub-divided into regional regiments, within which a number of smaller units known as battalions existed, divided into companies.

There would be many weeks of uncertainty about where Ballymena and its hinterland should be placed within the U.V.F.'s military geography and there was lack of clarity about the nomenclature and numbering of each battalion. However the men were finally filed under 'North Antrim Regiment' under the leadership of Sir Arthur O'Neill and in due course they were awarded the title '1st Battalion,' with George Young in command.

Inside the U.V.F. there was considerable room for individual battalions to foster their own culture and develop their own *esprit de corps*. In the months that lay ahead, Galgorm Castle would be at the centre of a concerted attempt to turn '1st N.A.R.' into one of the U.V.F.'s most competent battalions, attuned to the directives and needs of the Belfast leadership. And the Ulster Volunteers were now an ever-evolving, province-wide citizen army. They may well have reached the strength of 100,000 and more, by the summer of 1914.[122]

The commander for County Antrim as a whole was Sir William Adair. As a retired general with a set of high military standards he immediately indicated that he wanted to see big improvements in the men's drill, in their bearing and in such features of military etiquette as saluting superiors. The area which George Young was asked to 'command' initially included not only urban Ballymena but nine other 'districts' - Ahoghill, Buckna, Cullybackey, Glarryford, Portglenone, Broughshane, Carnalbanagh and Glenarm. In due course most of the men in the latter two areas were re-allocated to another U.V.F. regiment.[123]

Each Unionist Club was asked to register all members who wished to serve in the U.V.F. and these were divided into 'effectives' and 'non-effectives', the latter group consisting of men who through age, busyness or indisposition, could not offer active military service if conflict broke out. The term 'non-effective' should not be thought of as a disparaging one, even though 'non-effectives' were less integrated into the Ulster Volunteer project. In the local battalion they usually merited membership and a badge.[124]

In the latter part of January, Sir Arthur O'Neill, who now headed the North Antrim regiment, paid a visit to the Buckna Club. Of its 750 members, 120 had been to the Balmoral demonstration in the previous year and they had been well trained for that occasion but many other men had little experience of drill. Indeed the

---

122. Bowman, *Carson's Army*, p 1.

123. The Carnalbanagh and Glenarm districts would still appear to have still been part of the battalion in February 1913 (Mid-Antrim Museum, U.V.F. archive, MSMAB2011.34.1.14).

124. Reference to 'effectives' and 'non-effectives' appear often in the Mid-Antrim Museum, U.V.F. archives, where it is clear that badges are handed out to 'non-effectives' (Mid-Antrim Museum, U.V.F. archive, MSMAB2011.34.1).

Image 29. Local U.V.F. men practising drill in the courtyard of Galgorm Castle, the opulent home of the Young family, which was the epicentre of unionism in pre-war Mid-Antrim. (Young collection, Mid-Antrim Museum)

120 experienced volunteers had let their practice lapse in the winter months. O'Neill insisted that drill classes resume and he instigated a 'rifle club' to teach men 'how to shoot'.[125]

Also on the agenda was the process of weeding out men who lacked commitment or possessed an un-biddable character. In the words of the local leadership at a later juncture in the Home Rule Crisis, some men were to be 'struck off the roll' if they did not show discipline.[126] The battalions in the U.V.F. were at first divided into 'districts' and these 'districts' broken down into 'localities', with leaders chosen because they had the experience and the standing to train and command their men. Later, the 100-strong unit known as a company would become standard within the battalion. Amongst these leaders were several clergymen such as Reverend O.W. Clarke of Connor, who before long were training local men in the arts of soldiering.[127]

But the war of words also continued on public platforms in and around Ballymena, with an intensity born of the fact that Home Rule was now looming. Reverend Dr. McLaughlin from Armagh addressed the North End U.V.F. Club in January and launched into a full-scale attack on the Liberal Government, both for the Home Rule Bill and for other reforms such as the recent Insurance Act, in which employers had to contribute to health insurance schemes for lowly paid employees. McLaughlin felt that this placed too heavy a burden on Ulster employers and sapped their entrepreneurial morale.

---

125. *Ballymena Observer*, 31 January 1913.

126. Correspondence referencing members being 'struck off' (Mid-Antrim Museum, U.V.F. archive, MSMAB2011.34.1.27).

127. Details on the structuring of the U.V.F. and internal discipline appear in (Mid-Antrim Museum, U.V.F. archive during September-October 1913). See correspondence between General Adair and George Young and between Young and company commanders (Mid-Antrim Museum, U.V.F. archive, MSMAB2011.34.1.30-31 and MSMAB2011.34.1.40). By the autumn of 1913, a clear-cut and permanent company structure appears to have been in place. Clarke appears as an Ulster Volunteer leader throughout this archive and (P.R.O.N.I., O'Neill papers, D. 1238/2) where he is described as the commander of his local company within the 1st North Antrim battalion.

He also asserted that many nationalist agitators would be a curse to any country because of their work-shy mentality saying they were 'lazy, indolent and good for nothing and always sponging in or about a public house.' He considered many of them to be 'Molly Maguires', which was a term often used for members of secret and insurrectionary Irish brotherhoods.[128]

Opposition to the unionist project

The local industrialist and Liberal councillor John Dinsmore was on the attack. He wrote a letter to the *Observer* on 10th January to call the public's attention to the fact that he had been advocating separate Irish parliaments for the 'north-east' and the 'south' in Ireland since 1911 and that John Young had once poured scorn on this proposal and had called Dinsmore a 'poltroon'. Now, to Dinsmore's furious amusement, he saw that a similar model was being discussed by unionists at Westminster, who realised that the government was determined to pass their Home Rule Bill and that partition of the island might indeed be the only answer for Ulster. Thinking of the unionist leadership, he warned that 'history will reserve its severest condemnation for those quondam leaders who, blind to the ruthless march of events, have deliberately rejected counsels of prudence and ways of peace.' Then referring to a location in the Balkans where the Turkish troops had recently taken up a rearguard position to protect their capital city from the advancing enemy, Dinsmore claimed that unionist leaders had:

> 'led the Presbyterians of Ulster into the Chataldja lines of hopelessness and insensate resistance from which there is no honourable escape except by a foredoomed appeal to the iron dice, or else degrading and unconditional surrender.'[129]

As well as reading John Dinsmore's attack on unionism in the local papers, those Ballymena nationalists who purchased the Belfast-based daily paper, *Irish News*, would have been encouraged to learn about the outdoor concert at Glenarm on 25th January. The Clann Uladh band, also known as the 'War Pipers', had performed some of their most stirring pieces of music and a colourful standard was unfurled with the 'war-crest of the O'Neills emblazoned on it.' Amongst the tunes which the pipers played was the melody belonging to a famous song called *Tone's Grave*. This was a lament written by Thomas Davis for the leader of the United Irishmen, Wolfe Tone.[130] Tone had summoned French help for the insurgents of 1798 as they attempted to throw off British control. He had committed suicide when captured and his grave at Bodenstown in County Kildare had subsequently become a shrine for all committed nationalists:

> 'In Bodenstown churchyard there is a green grave
> And wildly around it the winter winds rave;
> Small shelter I ween are the ruined walls there
> When the storm sweeps down on the plains of Kildare.
> Once I lay on the sod that lies over Wolfe Tone
> And thought how he perished in prison alone,
> His friends un-avenged and his country un-freed.
> 'Oh bitter' I said 'is the patriot's meed.'

---

128. *Ballymena Observer*, 3 January 1913.

129. *Ballymena Observer*, 10 January 1913. The expression 'iron dice' was a not uncommon term during the 19th and early 20th centuries, referring to the 'gamble' of resorting to armed combat.

130. *Irish News*, 1 February 1913.

Meanwhile in *Irish News*, there was plenty of evidence for any Ballymena unionist who wished to dwell on the matter, that Irish Catholicism and Irish nationalism were thoroughly linked. The paper often featured a rich blend of advertisements for the Catholic Truth Society and articles about the robustly nationalist political grouping known as the United Irish League, which had considerable support all across Ireland and had often placed its emphasis on agrarian reform, including a subject that frightened rural Protestants - land redistribution. There was also regular news from the Ancient Order of Hibernians and a range of reports on pilgrimages to Lourdes, on the pages of *Irish News*.

Such material would have confirmed unionist suspicions of a looming Catholic hegemony under Home Rule. Anyone who read the paper on 27th January 1913 would have seen that Joseph O'Kane, the Ballycastle J.P. who had tackled Reverend Simpson about his heavily politicised religious views in the correspondence columns of the *Ballymena Observer*, was to be found delivering a lecture to the Catholic students of Queen's University, on the 'old but ever new motto of Faith and Fatherland.'[131]

Training the local Ulster Volunteer Force

By February 1913, opposition to Irish 'Faith and Fatherland' sentiments was growing apace in Mid-Antrim. Men with military experience stepped up to offer help with training the U.V.F. Robert Orr, whose family ran a successful legal firm, found more of his time being taken up with drilling the local volunteers, although he had been gazetted as an officer with the Somerset Light Infantry and, if European war were ever to break out, he would be obliged to leave at once for England.[132] By the end of the month, North End and Harryville Unionist Club members met for joint U.V.F. training exercises in which Orr played a key part. And by March and April 1913, the leaders of the local U.V.F. had recorded their first official lists of volunteers, noting their addresses and giving each man an 'organisation number.'[133]

During this time, rousing anti-nationalist speeches were being delivered at full volume by local clergy. During a meeting of the Mid-Antrim Unionist Women at Galgorm Parks, the Reverend Gilmour saw fit to re-iterate the judgment of his colleague the Reverend Simpson that Catholic nationalists were 'incapable of running this or any country.' He revisited the theme of papal perfidy, telling the ladies that 'Romanism' had 'blighted every country in which it had a ruling power.' And he re-worked the religious and political concept of Ireland, England and Scotland as a sacred trio, referring to these countries as a 'three-leafed shamrock' - while Wales, sadly, was once more overlooked in this trinitarian evocation of the Union. Gilmour warned that without this God-given union 'the grand old British Empire of theirs would totter into dust.'[134]

This was a time of feverish excitement. There were white-hot political issues for the older generation to discuss and a display of parades and military preparations for the young to enjoy on a weekly basis, either as participants or spectators. John Luke, who as an old man recorded his recollections of these earlier days, remembered being a small boy when Harryville was coming alive with loyalist street-theatre.

---

131. For mention of O'Kane's speech see *Irish News*, 27 January 1913.

132. For biographical information on Orr see the special wartime supplement to *Ballymena Observer*, 7 May 1915.

133. The Mid-Antrim Museum U.V.F. archive contains muster rolls for various local detachments of the organisation. These continued to be accumulated from 15 February 1913 until early in 1915. The U.V.F. 'locality leaders' generated these muster rolls and they were passed onto H.Q. in Belfast. In return each man was meant to be given an 'organisation number' (Mid-Antrim Museum, U.V.F. archive, MSMAB2011.33.1 and MSMAB2011.33.2).

134. *Ballymena Observer*, 25 April 1913.

Luke explained how local children had usually relied for fun on 'rolling old bicycle wheels' or playing 'marbles along the gutter', playing 'handball against somebody's gable wall' or else making wooden 'bogies' which were ridden down the slopes of a nearby hill at breathtaking speed. But now there were plenty of serious-looking older males to watch, who paraded in unison along the streets on their way back from long route-marches. Luke recalled one 'very sincere Loyalist' who was 'an oiler in the mill' and who often came up and down Queen street with a Lambeg drum:

> 'all the locals gathered in at night at his big peat fire. He bought his peats by the load and kept them upstairs. All the politics and situations pertaining to that particular time were discussed...'[135]

By May and June, with the arrival of warmth and sunshine, the Ballymena U.V.F. trained in the wide green spaces of Ballymena Demesne. As they marched, they were usually preceded by one of the town's loyalist bands. The sound of the martial music and the loud calls of the instructors to their troops became some of the most characteristic sounds during the summer of 1913, against the usual backdrop of mill-horns that signalled the beginning and end of Ballymena's factory shifts. Meanwhile, George Young and his immediate coterie of senior U.V.F. men handled an increased number of memos and instructions from the Ulster Volunteer Headquarters in Belfast. In June, one circular requested that 'armouries' be 'established in each battalion area' and that a suitable location should be found 'in the midst of and surrounded by Unionists.' The writer ordered that the number of guns which each battalion possessed should be recorded but kept publicly unknown.

Another circular stipulated that tests in drill and musketry must be undertaken and that certificates must be awarded on successful completion. The arms manual of the local British Army regiment, the Royal Irish Rifles, should be used in order to deliver professional training in the use of weaponry. Also in order to make the U.V.F. a more co-ordinated and efficient force in the event of conflict, four men in each company were to be given training in signalling, with an appropriate certificate presented at the conclusion of the course. During June a shooting competition was organised in the Harryville recreation grounds for the Ballymena U.V.F.[136]

Edward Carson and James Craig visit Ballymena, July 1913

Then as July approached, plans were made for the arrival of Sir Edward Carson, who would stay overnight, enjoying the hospitality at Galgorm Castle and meeting the loyalists of the district. June had been the first month in which Carson inspected the newly co-ordinated U.V.F. on a region-by-region basis and so the proposed military display at the show-grounds had to be undertaken to a high standard. Once again, as on Ulster Day, the council requested that businesses close and they asked residents to fly their flags.[137] At the '12th July' celebrations in Mid-Antrim, those who gathered for the annual parades no doubt discussed the even bigger event which lay ahead, when on the 18th of the month, Sir Edward would arrive into town at 1.30pm on the train from Belfast and find himself greeted as Ballymena's hero. In the absence as yet of the impressive uniforms that would start to make an appearance during the latter part of 1913, the Ulster Volunteers were instructed to 'wear dark clothes' and 'hard bowler hats' - not an easy request to make of

---

135. Eull Dunlop (ed.), John Luke's *Harryville*, (Ballymena, 1992) pp 9, 19, 27, 39, 44.

136. Information on armouries, basic drill training, signalling and musketry are located in correspondence between local command staff, divisional command staff and U.V.F. headquarters, February to October 1913 (Mid-Antrim Museum, U.V.F. archive, MSMAB2011.34.1.21, MSMAB2011.34.1.22 and MSMAB2011.34.1.39).

137. *Ballymena Observer*, 11 July 1913.

Image 30. A livestock mart in progress on the Fair Hill, Ballymena. In July 1913, a crowd heard Sir Edward Carson and James Craig speak and watched the 1st Battalion of the North Antrim Regiment on parade. (Mid-Antrim Museum collection)

some working-class men, who invariably wore cheap brimmed hats and could scarcely have afforded the purchase of a 'bowler'.[138]

Meanwhile, speeches from loyalist platforms on the 12th of July emphasised familiar ideological themes. Comparing Catholicism to the demonic paganism which Old Testament texts often depict, the Reverend Gilmour expressed relief and satisfaction that Ulster had not yet 'bowed the knee to Romish Baal' and congratulated the 'Christian heroes' in the unionist camp who were fighting for religious and political freedom.[139]

On 14th July, Sir Arthur O'Neill undertook a practice session with a group of local horsemen whom he had assembled as a small Ulster Volunteer cavalry unit, perhaps inspired by a desire to emulate a similar unit in Fermanagh, known as the Enniskillen Horse. O'Neill explained the routines required of them whilst they acted as a 'mounted guard' for Carson when he arrived later in the month. The former Life Guards officer was suited to the task of creating a ceremony such as this, because of the glamorous rituals played out by the Life Guards in the Household Cavalry, which had the job of accompanying the British monarch during important state occasions.[140]

---

138. Correspondence between Sir William Adair and George Young during June -July 1913 deals with plans for the arrival of Carson and Craig, for instance concerning the importance of wearing bowler hats and dark clothes, dated 18 July 1913 (Mid-Antrim Museum, U.V.F. archive, MSMAB2011.34.1.1-3).

139. *Ballymena Observer*, 18 July 1913.

140. See correspondence between Young, Adair and Sir Arthur O'Neill, in the Mid-Antrim Museum U.V.F. archive, concerning the plans for the leaders' visit including practice drill for the mounted guard (Mid-Antrim Museum, U.V.F. archive, MSMAB2011.34.1.1-3). The Enniskillen Horse is described in Bowman, *Carson's Army*, pp24, 50, 56, 83.

Four days later, the train that bore Edward Carson and James Craig to Ballymena set off on its journey, stopping at Antrim on the way, where the two leaders were met by a number of shipyard-workers who had made a journey from the city, to see the 'great man' and show him their support. Then the train moved on towards its destination, where the crowd that had gathered in and around the station heard loud reports from detonators that had been placed on the railway tracks, to create an impressively thunderous arrival. As the train slowed down beside the platform, the welcoming party could see Carson at the carriage window, politely lifting his hat to the onlookers. Then the two leaders stepped out of their luxurious saloon carriage, while all around the station, men and women sang their own version of a music-hall song that had become very popular during the last year:

'It's a long way to Ballymena
It's a long way to go...'

Image 31. Lapel badge created for Sir Edward Carson's visit to Mid-Antrim in July 1913. The lettering stresses not just his role as an M.P., but as a King's Council. He was one of the most distinguished lawyers of his generation and would become British attorney-general. (John Pattison collection)

Shaking hands with the welcoming party of unionist dignitaries, Carson and Craig emerged from the station to a loud cheer and were ushered into a horse-drawn carriage, alongside which Sir Arthur O'Neill's mounted guardsmen waited, several of whom were carrying ceremonial lances. Then, with great ceremony, the procession set off through streets which were festooned in flags and bunting along the route to Ballymena show-grounds, an urban scene which was a 'blaze of colour' as *Observer* enthusiastically noted. Several traditional loyalist arches had been erected along the route. Outside a number of shops and businesses, large painted slogans had been hoisted into position, including one sign outside the premises of Samuel Hood, which said 'WELCOME TO OUR LEADER'. There were also bowls of Orange lilies on display in many windows.

When the party arrived at the show-grounds to the sound of loud applause, the Ballymena Brass Band struck up 'For he's a jolly good fellow' until Carson mounted the platform. It seemed to a reporter from *Observer* that up to 20,000 people were either in the show-grounds or milling around outside. Meanwhile the U.V.F. had been marching towards the show-grounds from Ballymena Castle and they had timed their arrival perfectly. Over 600 troops entered the arena to a loud cheer and circled around the field, preceded by more horsemen of the 'mounted corps.'

They came to an abrupt halt in front of the platform-party, with a precision that impressed *Observer*'s reporter, 'nothing being wanted but the arms and the uniform, to constitute the turnout a splendid military force.'

Carson's speech was laced with the defiant rhetoric with which he had been inspiring crowds all across Ulster. He assured his Ballymena audience that while he was at the helm, unionists would never give in, nor would they compromise. Instead they would 'fight it out to the end' because they were convinced of the need to 'keep the old flag flying' over Ireland. Bursts of applause greeted his more vigorous oratorical flourishes, as when he told the Ballymena crowd 'there is no force on Earth which can conquer us.' And he spoke of his deep admiration for the Ulster Volunteers who were standing attentively before him: 'I don't think I have ever seen a finer body of men.' Then he added 'I want men who will follow me to the finish.'

Carson, like many unionist orators, was prone to utter dark warnings about the apocalypse that lay in waiting, which added greatly to the sense of existential crisis amongst Protestants and increased recruitment among them for the Ulster Volunteers. On this occasion he told his hearers that Home Rule would 'tear down the whole social fabric in England and in Scotland' and that it would 'breed hatreds and animosities which no man can measure.'

Image 32. A page from a scrapbook belonging to the Young family, portraying the visit of Carson and Craig, during which the elderly John Young of Galgorm Castle was a presiding figure and the Ballymena Horse provided a guard of honour. (Young collection, Mid-Antrim Museum)

Then his fellow M.P., James Craig, spoke to the crowd. He claimed that he 'would not rest content...till every man who called himself an Ulsterman was in the ranks of the Ulster Volunteer Force,' after which some people in the crowd shouted out, 'We are ready!'

Loud cheers once again broke out. However, the U.V.F. had been carefully instructed during the preceding days to show the steely calm that befits soldiers and to 'make no applause whatsoever' during the speeches. Then it was the turn of Sir Arthur O'Neill as the local M.P., to speak a few words to the crowd. He told them he was very satisfied that 'discipline' had been manifested amongst unionists in the local area and that there had been no 'disturbances', as had taken place in some other parts of Ulster. And he reminded his listeners that they should 'only resort to war if the forces of the Crown were ever employed against them to drive them out of the British parliament.'

The public meeting came to a close and a voice called out for 'three cheers' to be given for the speakers. Several days earlier, the local Ulster Volunteer officers had been instructed about proper etiquette for this moment, in a written circular which had specified that each man should show little overt emotion and simply 'wave his hat' and give 'three ringing cheers.' Then the National Anthem was sung, during which the U.V.F. men followed strict orders about etiquette and stood 'rigid to attention.' In due course, the two main speakers resumed the seats in their carriage at the heart of the mounted procession which made its way out of the town centre and along Galgorm Road towards the sylvan residence of the Young family. On their route to Galgorm they passed Norman Caruth's house, *Drumard*. An arch had been erected above the thoroughfare, on which two striking slogans were written: 'WHO WOULD BE FREE, THEMSELVES MUST STRIKE THE BLOW' and: 'ETERNAL VIGILANCE IS THE PRICE OF PEACE'.

Image 33. On the weekend of Craig and Carson's visit to Ballymena, they stayed with the Young family in the pastoral surroundings of Galgorm Castle, where deer wandered freely through the grounds. (Young collection, Mid-Antrim Museum)

At Galgorm Castle, Carson and Craig received warm hospitality, although it would appear that George Young's sister, Rose, kept a low profile during the weekend, recording the presence of Carson at her family home in a perfunctory manner within her daily diary. As for Willy Young's wife, Mary Alice, she would later record that she 'fell completely under his spell' but that it 'did not last.' Edward Carson was a gaunt, brooding and charismatic man who was capable of attracting personal admiration. However the reason for Mary Alice's later disillusion is not clear.

On the following day, Carson and Craig motored around the Ballymena area and met a variety of people. They arrived at the cattle market and were presented with a silver horseshoe, mounted on an ebony background. Arriving at Salisbury Square in Harryville, the unionist leaders met a loyalist called John Ellis, who presented them with a Bible which had been marked at a verse from St Paul's letter to the Romans: 'If the Lord be for us, who can be against us.' This was reputed to be the text that inspired the Protestant hero William of Orange on the eve of the Battle of the Boyne in 1690.

The unionist duo also toured the wider Ballymena hinterland, visiting Glenwherry, Buckna and Broughshane. Carson delighted his hearers at the last venue, when he told them that he had not yet 'read in history where Ulstermen were ever beaten.' After retiring once more to Galgorm Castle, the two men reappeared on Sunday, attending Ballymena 1st Presbyterian Church for morning worship at 12 noon. On Monday they took the train southwards to Whiteabbey.[141]

Unquestionably, the local treatment of Carson during the weekend had been imitative of the reception afforded to an emperor, in a town resplendent with flags and victory arches, through which armed horsemen accompanied him to a public arena where he could receive the adulation of his people. Although this was an age of regal and aristocratic pomp and circumstance, Ulster was actually very short on the cultured glamour of the dynastic families found in many European regions. Belfast lacked the social sophistication of Dublin, with its vice-regal lodge, its ancient castle, its magnificent and venerable university, its rich literary heritage and high - if contested - imperial status. Now that unionism was being prised apart from the Anglo-Irish culture of southern Protestants, many of whom had owned their estates for several centuries and possessed 'blue-blooded' lineage, there was clearly a need for a staged mimesis of regal tradition, for militaristic pageantry and for public rituals of honour and allegiance within the street-theatre that both embodied and generated Ulster's emerging unionist ideology.

Meanwhile, *Telegraph* continued to carry poetry to stir the heart of it readers. On 26th July, a poem appeared, which was written by an anonymous author, but possessed the regular rhythm and the buoyant, tendentious tone of a Rudyard Kipling ballad:

'Now we tell you we won't have it
And we mean it every man
And they say we've got to take it
You just make us if you can
We're a dour breed of Scotties
And we never play at bluff

---

141. For all details of Carson's and Craig's visit, see the extensive reports in *Ballymena Observer* and *Ballymena Weekly Telegraph* during July and August 1913. In particular, see the *Observer*, 11, 18, 25 July - the details of the leaders' itinerary and quotations from the speeches utilised in this account are located in the 25 July edition. Dunlop (ed.), *The Recollections of Mary Alice Young*, p 51, and the diaries of Rose Young, July 1913, contain brief comments on the visit of Carson to Galgorm.

And we're out for faith and freedom
And we're made of sterner stuff.

Now the Mollies they won't rule us
And we won't be sat upon
You may pass the word to Devlin
That we're ready - bring them on.
Lord bless our Ulster Army
And shield us in the fight
Then forward boys and steady -
Take your dressing from the right.'[142]

Image 34. A souvenir bust of Sir Edward Carson with a Ballymena crest. Mass-production of loyalist souvenirs, postcards and regalia was one the key features of the Home Rule Crisis.
(Mid-Antrim Museum collection)

The composition of Buckna rural U.V.F. unit

But as 1913 drew on, there were those like Edward Carson who foresaw deep trouble ahead. An editorial comment in the *Observer* - probably penned by editor and North End Unionist Club member John Wier - expressed great concern that 'Ireland is drifting to the edge of a cataract.'[143]

Anxiety was perhaps increased by the fact that the local U.V.F. was an ever more noticeable public presence, sharpening everyone's anticipation of a possible confrontation with the police, the British Army and nationalists. Directives from Ulster Volunteer headquarters had ordered local regional leaders to make their troops more militarily versatile. So men were asked to seek permission from employers to go on 'night-time marches' in order to participate in simulations of nocturnal warfare as part of the training expected in any competent army. Daylight route marches from Ballymena to Ahoghill and back, and also from Ballymena to

---

142. *Ballymena Weekly Telegraph*, 26 July 1913.

143. *Ballymena Observer*, 29 August 1913.

Broughshane and back, occupied the Ballymena U.V.F. on Tuesday evenings during August and September.[144]

Whereas the Ballymena units of the Ulster Volunteers clearly contained many men who worked on factory floors and at shop counters throughout the day, the units which had been formed in rural Mid-Antrim had a different social composition. There are a number of incomplete but informative records of Ulster Volunteer membership in both rural and urban vicinities within the local U.V.F. archive. Records for the Buckna area reveal quite a lot about the Ulster Volunteers within a rural context. A number of men who in the 1911 census had been described as 'farmers', 'farmer's sons' and 'agricultural labourers' were enrolled as members. The overwhelming denominational ethos of the unit was Presbyterian, though one U.V.F. man's Roman Catholic mother-in-law lived in the house with him, his wife and their children. Another man who lived with his widowed sister, is described in the census as belonging to the 'Christian Brethren'.

The social and economic status of these volunteers varied considerably. One man was designated a 'woollen manufacturer' in the census returns. Another man - a middle-aged agricultural labourer denoted as possessing poor literacy skills - would have depended through most of his life on daily employment on neighbouring farms. There was also an artisan designated as a 'master carpenter' within the ranks of the Buckna U.V.F. and a farmer's son who would seem to have inherited a considerable level of prosperity. The census returns show that his father owned a piggery, a cow house, a calf house, a fowl house, a barn and a shed.

It may be assumed that men of higher social rank were more likely to take on leadership roles but in a location such as Buckna, with a well-established agricultural tradition, there was a weaker history of soldiering in the ranks of the British army than in Irish towns or in those remote or barren rural areas of Ireland which endured endemic poverty. As a result, there would have been a heavy reliance on any old 'army man' who could be found to deliver some rudimentary training or any middle-class professionals who resided in the surrounding district and who, when undertaking their university education, may have been members of an army cadet unit or an officer training corps. It should be recognised that local clergy, as university or seminary graduates, were quite likely to have been members of such units as younger men, which helps explain the presence of men such as the Reverend O.W. Clarke in the officer corps of the Mid-Antrim U.V.F.

There was a wide range of ages amongst the Buckna men. Some men were in their mid-sixties and would have had no active role to play in future warfare. There were young lads on the muster-rolls who were aged just 14 and 15. While the presence of boys who would now be classed as 'teenagers' may indicate that the Ulster Volunteers were to some degree made up of 'boy soldiers', it should be remembered that at 14 years of age, both males and females were already doing a long day's work in the mills and the fields of Mid-Antrim.

However 14 and 15-year-olds were no longer allowed to join the 20th century British Army as they had often done in previous centuries. During the Great War this rule preventing the enlistment of 'boy soldiers' officially applied but, as is now widely known, under-age lads did manage to make it through the enlistment process and subsequently fought and died in the trenches.

It is also clear that in a rural area such as Buckna, where members of the U.V.F. were scattered over a wide area of countryside, assembling the men for drill sessions, marches and lectures would have been much more of a challenge than in the towns, where an entire U.V.F. unit may well have lived in a series of adjacent streets.

144. Memoranda regarding the need for training routines is located in (Mid-Antrim Museum, U.V.F. archive, MSMAB2011.34.1.40). See too correspondence between Robert Robert Orr and his superiors (Mid-Antrim Museum, U.V.F. archive, MSMAB2011.34.1.47). See also regular articles regarding U.V.F. route marches in both local papers throughout the late summer and autumn of 1913, for instance the marches which took place on 26 August and 2 September.

And whereas the shifts in a factory presented a constant routine throughout the year, a farm labourer's job involved unpredictable pressures in terms of emergency care for livestock and seasonal variations in labour.

Training rural volunteers and conveying them to public events in Ballymena would thus have been a difficult enterprise.[145]

The 1st Battalion of the U.V.F. North Antrim Regiment begins to take shape

Gradually, from September though to December, the re-organisation of U.V.F. nomenclature and structure was completed and '1st N.A.R.' was now being divided into a coherent series of 'companies' which, according to the records held by Sir Arthur O'Neill, were classified as follows:

A Company – recruiting in Ballymena and operating from the North End club rooms, with a commander called R. Baird, from 7, Albert Place.

B Company – recruiting in Ballymena and operating out of the same location, with a commander called R. Pryde, who resided at *Leighinmor*.

C Company – recruiting in Harryville (including Ballymarlow, Slaght and Tullygarley) and operating out of the Harryville reading rooms, with a commander called S. McFetridge, of 34, Castle Street.

D Company – recruiting in The Braid (including Raceview, Buckna and Skerry), and operating out of Raceview, with a commander called J.K. Wilson, who lived in Raceview.

E Company – One half company was recruited in Cullybackey. One half company was drawn from Hillmount. The entire company operated out of Hillmount, with Commander T.G. (Tommy) Haughton in charge.

F Company – One half company came from Glenwherry. One half company came from Craigywarren. They operated out of Craigywarren Orange Hall, with their commander being William Wallace of Engine Row, Ballygarvey.

G Company – Ahoghill, Portglenone, Galgorm and Gracehill, operating out of Galgorm Castle, under commander W.R. (Willy) Young of Kintullagh.

H Company – recruiting in Clough and operating out of Clough Orange Hall, with a commander called Reverend Charles Stanley-Stewart, of Clough.

J Company – Recruiting in Connor, operating out of Connor Orange Hall, with Commander Reverend O.W. Clarke, of Connor in charge.

---

145. Muster-rolls for the Buckna area, taken from the Mid-Antrim Museum U.V.F. archive, have been interpreted using the Census for Ireland 1911. The rolls appear to have been completed, added to and revised during February, March, September and December. The muster–rolls for companies recruiting in urban Ballymena reveal a predictable mix of workers in factories, in the transport network, at the markets and in local shops as well as those who were in clerical and professional occupations. The historian's ability to create reliable statistics about the social composition and size of the 1st Battalion of the North Antrim Regiment from these muster-rolls is greatly hampered by the fact that they were written and sometimes re-written at a variety of different times by a variety of authors who are often anonymous and do not specify whether or not the persons on the lists became active and sustained members of the organisation.

K Company – Recruiting in the vicinity described as 'Newtown Crommelin', operating out of 'Newtown Crommelin' Orange Hall, with no commander as yet appointed by the end of 1913.

Half Company commanders included S. McGarry, J. Nelson, T. Wilson, A. Montgomery, R. McNeill, W. McKelvey, N. (Norman) Carruth of *Drumard*, W.G. Flynn, R. Walker, A. Bell, and F. Marshall.

Those leaders who had originally operated as locality officers asked their men to elect their new company commanders and half-company commanders. In that sense the U.V.F. had a degree of democratic internal governance that was quite different from the 'top-down' hierarchy of the British Army. Each company was built up of twelve-strong squads, with two squads in a section, two sections in a half company and two half companies in a full company. The total number for each company, including officers, was meant to come to approximately one hundred men. As a result '1st N.A.R.' was aiming to operate with a full strength of over a 1,000 'effective' volunteers.

As this account will show, some companies must have gathered in many more 'effectives' than this. There were also hundreds of other men who were capable of contributing in practical ways to the U.V.F. cause as 'non-effectives', through providing food, transport, accommodation or a trade such as vehicle maintenance, although this was a rather more diffuse and loosely affiliated group. Some local women wished, in this era of radical gender politics, to play an active role in the Ulster Volunteer movement, as signallers, telegraphists or nurses, although they would appear to have been mainly confined to nursing duties within the Mid-Antrim area.

Metal lapel badges for the province-wide U.V.F. had been manufactured by the second half of 1913 and they were handed out on a county by county basis. Each volunteer, whether as an 'effective' or otherwise, received a badge inscribed with a letter that signified the unit to which he belonged and a personal 'organisation number.' Correspondence in the Ballymena U.V.F. archive describes how canvas armlets had also been mass-produced for the Ulster Volunteers, in khaki for the men in the ranks and in red for most of the U.V.F. officers.[146]

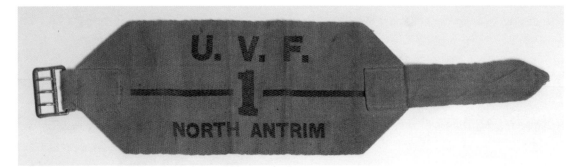

Image 35. The armband of an Ulster Volunteer in the 1st Battalion, North Antrim Regiment of the U.V.F., to which most local volunteers belonged. Committed volunteers were also issued with badges.
(John Pattison collection)

---

146. Many details about the local battalion of the Ulster Volunteers during 1913 and 1914, including internal structure, governance, numbering, badges and armlets and company strength found in (Mid-Antrim Museum, U.V.F. archive, MSMAB2011.34.1.6, 15, 22). References to women in the Mid-Antrim U.V.F. project are primarily to do with nursing care (Mid-Antrim Museum, U.V.F. archive, MSMAB2011.34.1.49-61). The most authoritative summary of the battalion structure with its leadership details, which is reprinted here, is to be found in (P.R.O.N.I., O'Neill papers, D. 1238/2). Further details on the structure of the U.V.F. at a national level are found in Bowman, *Carson's Army*, chapters three and five.

The beginnings of the Irish National Volunteers

To the alarm of the British government, the U.V.F. was not the only group of men marching the roads of Ireland by the end of 1913. In Dublin, since January, a group of nationalists had been practising military formation in premises in Parnell Square, led by men who had had a background in the secret society known as the Irish Republican Brotherhood. By the summer they had devised a strategy for generating a large nationalist militia not dissimilar to the Ulster Volunteer Force. Part of the plan involved finding a highly regarded and 'respectable' public figure to be the leader of their cause and the man they won over was the renowned academic, Professor Eoin MacNeill. He was a History Professor in Dublin and although he had no interest in insurrectionary strategies, he became convinced of the need for a militia that would protect the interests of resurgent Irish nationalism and prevent the project of a reconstituted Dublin parliament from slipping out of Ireland's grasp. By mid-November, a first meeting of the Irish Volunteers took place in the Irish capital. Within the next few months, units of the new organisation were springing up in County Antrim, as in every other Irish county. Amongst those who were likely to join or at least deliver sympathy and support, were members of the Ancient Order of Hibernians, the Gaelic Athletic Association and Irish cultural enthusiasts in the Gaelic League. A branch of the Gaelic League existed in Ballymena.[147] Open conflict between the two militias did not emerge in County Antrim in the last two months of 1913, but there was potential for it to do so, even in such quiet, idyllic locations as the small towns that dotted the Antrim coast.

In Glenarm, which was MacNeill's birthplace, nationalists and unionists existed side by side. Given the existence of an overt nationalist culture in the town, as described in an earlier part of this narrative, a company of the Irish Volunteer movement was undoubtedly being formed by the end of the year. Yet this was the town where, each Monday evening, a unit of the Ulster Volunteer Force went on a route march. On 10th November, for instance, the Glenarm U.V.F. men marched towards Carnlough and back, listening all the while to the Irish Sea which rushed ashore in the darkness, just a few yards from the famously scenic coastal road. As one of the Ulster Volunteers told a reporter for the *Observer*, 'the night was beautifully clear and very favourable for the purpose.' Yet how rival groupings of Irish and Ulster Volunteers would handle the situation, should they meet one another in the darkness, was anybody's guess.[148]

Caution, scepticism and opposition - some Protestant reactions to militarised unionism

To some Ballymena clergy, the situation now looked very perilous. Canon Ross called out in his sermons for calm and earnestness. He pleaded, 'that nothing may be done by any party to leave behind any lasting root of bitterness' or that would start a series of 'prolonged vindictive reprisals.' He suggested that local political leaders should learn humility and that they might begin by 'endeavouring to see where we have been wrong in the past'. Ross argued that 'a man may be convinced of the truth of his own convictions...of the righteousness of the position he has taken up...' but that 'he and his party have sometimes been wrong and may go wrong again...'

---

147. Detailed accounts of the emergence and organisation of the Irish National Volunteers in the north of the island are scarce but very brief accounts of the I.N.V. may be found in such histories of the period as Lee, *Ireland 1912-85, Politics and Society*, pp 14-24. See too the range of essays included in F.X. Martin, *The Irish Volunteers 1913-1915* (Dublin, 1963). The local Gaelic League branch is mentioned in *Ballymena Weekly Telegraph*, 8 October 1913.

148. The Glenarm U.V.F. route march received coverage in *Ballymena Observer*, 14 November 1913.

He warned that:

> 'there may be a time coming when calmness and steadiness in the community and the individual may prove of enormous importance: when hastiness and temper and passion may have it in their power to do irreparable harm...the danger is very real and very near...'[149]

However Ross did not engage in open disagreement with the Covenant project or with the U.V.F. These steps were taken by his fellow cleric F.J. MacNeice in Carrickfergus, several miles to the south of Ballymena. Whilst MacNeice was not an Irish nationalist, he did regard the tactics of the unionist leadership as socially divisive, ill-judged and likely to end in communal violence. He proceeded to share his views with his congregation in a number of sermons that seem to have been received with polite scepticism.[150]

Image 36. The former facade of Wellington Street Presbyterian Church, Ballymena. The minister, Reverend Gilmour, was an ardent spokesman for the unionist cause, as were most Protestant clerics in this era. U.V.F. church services were a regular occurrence in Ballymena, during which collections were taken up for the equipment fund. (Mid-Antrim Museum collection)

For Rose Young the growing overlap of support for the Irish language and membership of this new nationalist militia would have added to the discomfort of being part of an Ulster Volunteer household. And increasing

---

149. *Ballymena Observer*, 3 October 1913.

150. There is coverage of MacNeice's attitudes to unionism in Scholes, *The Church of Ireland and the Third Home Rule Bill*, (Dublin, 2010), p 60-61.

the difficulty for Rose was the knowledge that her relative Roger Casement had become ever more outspoken in his nationalism. On learning of the existence of the Irish Volunteers, he was filled with fresh enthusiasm. Before long he was corresponding with the I.N.V. leadership, expressing satisfaction that the Home Rule crisis had set Ulster Protestants on a road towards conflict with the Britain that they claimed to serve. Casement had already proclaimed his desire to 'light a fire' that would 'set the Antrim hills ablaze,' destroy sectarianism and 'unite' the people of Ireland, irrespective of their religion.[151]

But the Irish Volunteers were accompanied onto the stage of 20th century Irish history by another much smaller militia with strong connections to the Mid-Antrim gentry. Captain Jack White had been a guest of Rose Young at Galgorm Castle on several occasions. His views would already have been deemed deeply disloyal by local unionists, knowing that he regarded them as guilty of 'pseudo-Protestant political popery.'[152] But now this 'black sheep' son of the Ladysmith hero, Sir George White, was becoming even more of a menace. Closely involved with Jim Larkin in the Irish Transport and General Workers' Union strike in Dublin which began in August, White suggested to Larkin that a small 'Irish Citizens' Army' (I.C.A.) should be formed to protect the interests and well-being of the strikers and their families. This was a pre-emptive strategy, undertaken in the light of the role played by the British Army in suppressing the famous dockers' strike which had taken place six years previously in Belfast.

Image 37. A slouch hat belonging to the Irish Citizens' Army. Hats of a similar style constituted the head-dress of the local U.V.F. Battalion. Both militias also shared the motif of the Red Hand of Ulster. (Item on display in Mid-Antrim Museum - on loan from the National Museum of Ireland)

---

151. Comments by Casement found in Dudgeon, *Roger Casement - the Black Diaries*, p 404.

152. White, *Misfit*, p 113.

At a meeting of strikers in Clontarf he endeavoured to set up a military structure and enrol men into companies and battalions, with officers and N.C.O.s. Then, out of his own money - very possibly enriched by the proceeds of the will of his recently deceased father - he purchased pairs of boots and some other equipment for this embryonic revolutionary militia. He received plenty of encouragement from Casement as he began this task. Casement sent a brief, tersely worded but enthusiastic telegram to White: 'Strongly approve proposed drill and discipline Dublin workers.'

Casement indicated that he believed the recruiting and training of the U.V.F. had set an excellent example of the kind of militarisation that was needed in Ireland. However, White began to feel disillusioned with his colleagues in the Labour movement and he was perturbed to see boots that he had purchased for his men end up in the local pawn shops. Notoriously volatile, he eventually quit the Dublin labour scene in 1914, although the militia that he had devised did not die and under the leadership of the Marxist activist and writer James Connolly, the I.C.A. raised its distinctive flag known as the Starry Plough and continued to recruit.[153]

Image 38. A replica tunic belonging to the Irish Citizens' Army. The first set of uniforms for this militia was paid for by Captain Jack White, son of the Boer War hero, Sir George White V.C. of Broughshane. The militia would eventually take part in the Easter Rising during 1916. (Item on display in Mid-Antrim Museum - on loan from the National Museum of Ireland)

In October, White devoted himself to the organisation of a meeting in Ballymoney, which was focused on attracting Irish Protestants who dissented from unionism and who regarded the arrival of Home Rule with few qualms. The event took place on 24th October and attracted several hundred people to the town hall to hear Sir Roger Casement, Reverend J.B. Armour, Jack White himself and a few other speakers, who proceeded to deliver the case for an Irish parliament and assert that unionists were fomenting communal hate.

A liberal critique of Ballymena's unionist leaders

John Dinsmore had already voiced public disdain for the current unionist project and he proved to be the most vigorous and controversial speech-maker on the night of the meeting in Ballymoney, although he appears to have spoken from the floor rather than the platform. It seems that he had been warned by an

153. The careers of White and Casement and the development of the I.C.A. are explained in White, *Misfit*, pp113-181. Casement's comments are located on pp164, 167. The diaries of Rose Young often reveal evidence of social relationship with the White and Casement families, for instance on 12 November 1913.

unnamed source not to attend, as Ballymena's 'Protestant home rulers' were not a popular species and there might be violent reprisals. But rather than lessening Dinsmore's enthusiasm for the event, the warning would seem to have emboldened him. It is clear from local newspaper accounts that he spoke out against 'the great linen magnates' for what he saw as the manipulation of sectarianism in order to distract workers from what he called 'poverty wages'. Possibly reworking a phrase of Christ's from the Gospels, Dinsmore suggested that when these hungry workers 'asked for bread they were given Boyne Water.'

The Ballymoney solicitor Thomas Taggart, who was an organiser of the meeting, would later record that Dinsmore thought he had been 'shot at' on his return to that 'impossible' town of Ballymena. Taggart seemed to think that this was not an attempt to kill Dinsmore but rather a 'prank,' involving a firework.

Quite undeterred, Dinsmore engaged in correspondence with political opponents in the letter columns of *Telegraph* during the ensuing weeks. He launched straight into an alliterative attack on the 'bias and the bitterness of pumped up partisanship for party and self-serving ends'. He condemned the kind of political leader who, in his opinion, played around with a fabricated civilian army but was in reality a 'sneaking coward, plotting from behind a hedge'. He accused such men of 'drilling invertebrate volunteers' and 'opening quite unnecessary Orange Halls' and he denounced this behaviour sarcastically as 'a splendid solution for hungry mouths and insanitary hovels'.

He argued that in the linen spinning mills outside Belfast, the average wage was nine shillings and three pence per week and that although this was a 14% rise from seven years ago, the cost of living had gone up by 20% in that time. He pointed out that wages in his own woollen manufacturing business had risen to thirteen shillings, six pence and a halfpenny during this period. There was a real likelihood, he contended, of the Ulster linen merchants being taken to task by the Trade Board for operating a system of 'sweated labour.'

A lively argument soon developed in *Telegraph*, in which a couple of Dinsmore's critics accused him of being a less generous employer than he claimed, particularly at a new factory which he had opened at Ahoghill. One critic suggested that Dinsmore was self-righteously painting himself as a latter day St Francis of Assissi, the man who had been known as the 'little friend of the poor.' His response was to fire back further epistolary salvos, saying that he was very glad to be associated with someone as benign as St Francis and backing up his arguments about the exploitative nature of the linen industry with statistics taken from the Labour Gazette. He proclaimed that:

'the linen lords of Ballymena and Belfast paid a man one shilling to beat the bigotry drum to keep the workers at variance in order to get their work done for a low wage.'

Dinsmore went on to praise the Liberal government in Westminster, saying that:

'if the working men of Ulster would only use the intelligence that God gave them and look below the empty shibboleths and immemorial antipathies they are mind-fed with, they would realise who are their true friends, as their fellow workers in England and Scotland have realised long ago.'

He also claimed that 'we employers must pay better wages if the workers are to remain in the country...' and 'I shall be glad and proud to pay more.' Then he added that economic decline was beginning to set in and that County Antrim was 'steadily and ruthlessly going down' and all the while the 'poor souls' who would suffer most from that decline were trotting 'after that ancient herring' of loyalism.

Writing his letters in a somewhat messianic frame of mind, Dinsmore suggested that he was, like a certain well-known religious teacher 'stoned by the Jews and Pharisees...for trying to open the poor man's eyes.' His final comment in the letter columns came on 6th December when he noted that linen workers' wages had indeed been raised since the Ballymoney meeting but that no-one should be conned into thinking that the big magnates of the textile industry were now melting with generosity:

> 'The linen lords of Ulster are not out for loyalty, they are out for loot...these modern buccaneers are rifling, not the places of the wealthy but the unprotected places of the poor.'[154]

Training and rhetoric intensify within Ballymena's unionist community

Adding to the pain of this sustained critique by Dinsmore, local unionists were facing the grim reality that King George V showed no sign of refusing to sign the Home Bill. As a faithful servant of the cause, the Reverend Gilmour had already poured out his heart in public during the first anniversary of Ulster Day. He had told his audience that he was searching for 'heavenly wisdom' amidst 'national perplexity' and he had publicly lamented yet again, the 'malicious and cruel designs of the foe.' He had asked:

> 'Is it too much to expect the Protestant King of a Protestant Nation to take his stand for national righteousness? Surely not, surely not!'

He had decried in customary fashion the 'image worship' of Catholicism and the remorseless way in which 'Romanists' profaned the Sabbath whilst their clergy promoted 'error and superstition' amongst the Irish people. Mixing his metaphors somewhat, Gilmour had told his audience:

> 'we have been planted in this land to keep the light burning...[despite] the wolves of Nationalism and Romanism.'

Adding to the sense of crisis, there was also a threat of industrial unrest among Ballymena's otherwise loyal workers and the fear that John Dinsmore's analysis of industrial relations might be germane. In recent weeks, the carters and porters on whom the commercial life of the town depended had gathered at Harryville Bridge, seeking better wages in keeping with their colleagues all across the country. Their demands were met very generously with wage rises of approximately 20% and the matter was settled. But which would be the next set of workers to engage in industrial action?[155]

Meanwhile, directives either from U.V.F. headquarters in Belfast or from Sir William Adair's county office kept pouring into Galgorm Castle. On 1st November, Adair asked George Young for submission of a list of 'medical gentlemen' who might be suitable for deployment as 'battalion surgeons.' A few days later, he requested that Young and his staff gather in 'blankets, great coats, boots, canteens, knives, forks, spoons, haversacks, tents' in preparation for extended manoeuvres and the overnight 'camps of instruction' which were beginning to appear in the U.V.F. leadership's itinerary.

---

154. The story of Dinsmore's participation in the Ballymoney meeting and his correspondence on the topics of Home Rule, unionism and sectarianism are contained in *Ballymena Weekly Telegraph* throughout October, November and December 1913, in particular 15, 29 November and 6 December. For details on the 'shooting' see also *Irish News*, 13 November 1913 and the correspondence of Thomas Taggart (National Library of Ireland, Casement Papers, N.L.I. 13073/15). The papers of J.B. Armour are located in (P.R.O.N.I., J.B. Armour, D.1792).

155. For Gilmour's comments and details of local industrial unrest, see *Ballymena Weekly Telegraph*, 4 October 1913.

Image 39. A crowd gathers in the Protestant Hall on the Galgorm Road in Ballymena to hear anti-Home Rule speeches. The venue was commonly packed for political meetings during this period. (Image courtesy of the *Ballymena Observer*)

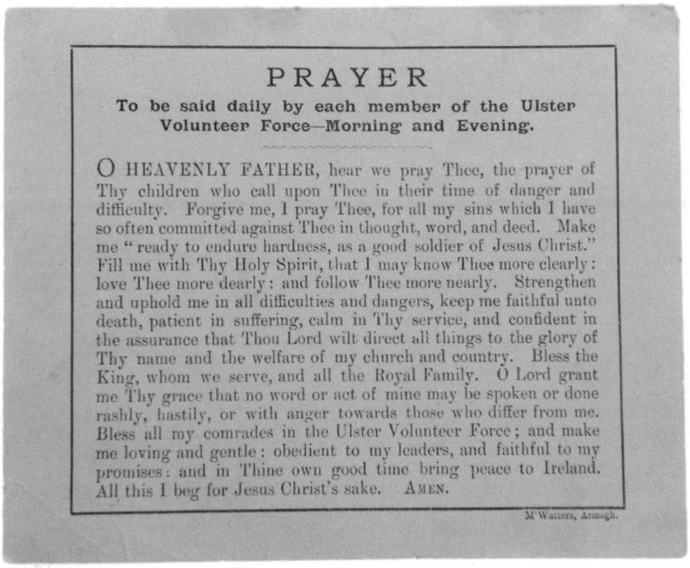

> ### PRAYER
> #### To be said daily by each member of the Ulster Volunteer Force—Morning and Evening.
>
> O HEAVENLY FATHER, hear we pray Thee, the prayer of Thy children who call upon Thee in their time of danger and difficulty. Forgive me, I pray Thee, for all my sins which I have so often committed against Thee in thought, word, and deed. Make me "ready to endure hardness, as a good soldier of Jesus Christ." Fill me with Thy Holy Spirit, that I may know Thee more clearly: love Thee more dearly: and follow Thee more nearly. Strengthen and uphold me in all difficulties and dangers, keep me faithful unto death, patient in suffering, calm in Thy service, and confident in the assurance that Thou Lord wilt direct all things to the glory of Thy name and the welfare of my church and country. Bless the King, whom we serve, and all the Royal Family. O Lord grant me Thy grace that no word or act of mine may be spoken or done rashly, hastily, or with anger towards those who differ from me. Bless all my comrades in the Ulster Volunteer Force; and make me loving and gentle: obedient to my leaders, and faithful to my promises: and in Thine own good time bring peace to Ireland. All this I beg for Jesus Christ's sake. AMEN.
>
> M'Watters, Armagh.

Image 40. A prayer card belonging to an Ulster Volunteer. These cards were distributed by the Church of Ireland to its U.V.F. members. Leaders of the U.V.F. and many ordinary volunteers saw themselves as part of a well-disciplined Christian militia which was doing God's will in Ireland. (John Pattison collection)

They were a suitable way of training key members to do something more worthwhile than supervise endless sessions of drill.

In fact there was disquiet among the senior leaders of 1st N.A.R. that the good standards manifested during Sir Edward Carson's visit had slipped away. On 5th December, Robert Orr wrote a letter to the Ballymena company commanders indicating that the men responded in an inadequate way to their commands and that their saluting was 'sloppy.' He told them that he couldn't allow this to be a 'go as you please regiment.' General Adair was also unhappy. He complained that throughout the regimental area 'a large number of men...have not presented themselves for training, and...will probably never become efficient...' He was also worried that too much time was devoted to the wrong kind of training for the men. Precious time should be:

> 'utilised in preparing them for tactical operations; accuracy in parade movements being of minor importance.'

This signalled a change in U.V.F training in the months that lay ahead, with an emphasis on 'battlefield' situations, logistics, the garnering of supplies, the procurement and storage of arms and close surveillance of the 'enemy.'[156] And meanwhile the background noise of clerical speech-making continued unabated. In November, the Methodist cleric, Reverend J.D. Ritchie took part in an Orange gathering in Ballymena and assured his audience that despite the bad news on the Home Rule front, everyone should feel cheered by the 'fact' that the Catholic church did not have a future. He told his audience that 'that vast system of tyranny and demoralisation is doomed'.

However, Protestants must 'refrain', he said, 'from all uncharitable words, actions, or sentiments towards Roman Catholics.' Ritchie was not out of line with other Methodists in Ulster, who tended to share the anti-Home Rule sentiments of their fellow-Protestants in the Presbyterian and Church of Ireland denominations.[157]

Training continued and Robert Orr continued his hard work with A, B and C companies of the U.V.F. who trained on Tuesday nights under powerful gas lamps in the 'Linenhall drill yard.' 'Commander Orr', as he was now known, surveyed the proceedings on horseback. A few days later, the men were present when a handsome blue banner was unfurled, which had been made from silk. It was ringed with gold and bore the badge of the Unionist Clubs of Ireland on one side. On the other side there were two inscriptions - 'Ballymenagh of the Seven Towers' and 'Ulster Volunteer Force, presented by Lady Annabel O'Neill, 1913'. Lady O'Neill and her husband were both present and Sir Arthur made a short speech in which he attempted to rally the spirits of everyone by suggesting that the letters 'U.V.F.' stood for 'Ulster's Victory Flag.'[158]

Then on 15th December there was an evening inspection of 1st N.A.R. by Sir William Adair at the Fair Hill, under floodlights. To the sound of a bugle, the men came to attention as Adair arrived. The Ballymena Brass Band and Seven Towers Flute Band played while the battalion marched past the general in columns and quarter columns. This was followed by close inspection of drill. Despite his earlier advice about focusing the U.V.F. on strategy and logistics, Adair was still a stickler for good drill. He had sent a note out on the first of

156. See the correspondence between George Young and Sir William Adair and between local U.V.F. leadership and H.Q. in Belfast, October - December, 1913. (Mid-Antrim Museum, U.V.F. archive, MSMAB2011.34.1.46-47).

157. *Ballymena Observer*, 14 October 1913. See *Ballymena Weekly Telegraph* for 16 March 1912, for details of a Methodist Convention in which disapproval of Home Rule was expressed.

158. *Ballymena Observer*, 28 November 1913.

Image 41. Ulster Volunteers from a Ballymena family. The group includes a young man who is a bugler for his company, comprising at least 100 men. Bugling was a common feature of uniformed organisations in this period, including the Boys' Brigade. (John Pattison collection)

the month to say that all 'effectives' must complete ten good drill sessions to be worthy of their badge and their armlets, of which 1,382 had been ordered for the battalion by early December.[159]

One minor controversy had developed in late November, when it emerged that the District Nursing Society had been giving instructions to local U.V.F. units. At a meeting of the society on twenty-fourth of the month, the committee insisted that any classes offered by members must be 'open to all and carried out on a non-political and non-sectarian basis.' The commitment of local unionist women had certainly grown and a signalling class had even been set up for those who were interested, in the hope that their skills would be acknowledged by the men-folk. In fact a 'Working Women's Unionist Group' had also been initiated to encourage females from the 'lower' social ranks to help in any way they could, learning basic nursing skills and supporting their Ulster Volunteer men-folk at all times.[160]

159. See *Ballymena Observer*, 12, 19, December 1913 and correspondence between Sir William Adair and George Young, November-December 1913 (Mid-Antrim Museum, U.V.F. archive, MSMAB2011.34.1.77).

160. *Ballymena Observer*, 24 October, 28 November, 5 December 1913.

The Christmas season brought festivity and light relief as usual. By 27th December the snow began to fall and the temperature dropped. On the last night of the year, Rose Young recorded 20 degrees of frost at Galgorm in her diary.[161] Two days beforehand, her brother had passed on Carson's instructions to his company leaders, asking them to distribute new information to their men, early in the new year.

The note read:

> 'Let there be more secrecy and less confidential relations with the authorities. Let them tell the press less and let them keep their own counsels more.'[162]

It was becoming clear to men like Young, that the loyalist project was going to have to delve deeper into conspiracy in its attempt to thwart Home Rule and that victory, if it were to be obtained at all, would come at a cost.

161. The diaries of Rose Young, 31 December 1913.

162. Correspondence between U.V.F. H.Q. in Belfast and George Young's office, 29 December 1913 (Mid-Antrim U.V.F. archive, MSMAB2011.34.2.5).

Chapter Four

1914 - The Year of the Guns

Chapter Four
1914 - The Year of the Guns

Motorcars, cavalry, rations and signals - expanding the capacity of the Mid-Antrim U.V.F.

By the early weeks of 1914, George Young was caught up in a fresh whirlwind of activity as directives arrived thick and fast from Belfast H.Q. and from his two immediate seniors in the U.V.F., Sir Arthur O'Neill and Sir William Adair. One of the first items to arrive was a province-wide instruction, asking for a list of motor vehicles. These vehicles had to be available in the event of a military emergency. A note had to be taken of whether the owner would permit local or wider usage and whether he or she would permit a 'careful expert driver' from a local 'garage' to take charge of the car.

Amongst those who volunteered his vehicle was J.K. Wilson of Raceview, the commander of D company and the owner of a sleek-looking four-seater Touring Rover Turpido, manufactured by the prestigious Bugatti Company. Wilson stressed that the Turpido must be used only within the Mid-Antrim area. By 10th February, the Haughton family had offered their five-seater Humber and wished to supply a professional driver. The Humber was a smart-looking vehicle, with canvas roof, prominent headlights and a set of spare wheels fastened to the sides of the vehicle. The Haughtons hoped that 'a day's notice' would be given before the car's procurement, but suggested that the vehicle would be available within 'several hours if absolutely necessary.'[163]

In the first few months of 1914, U.V.F. 'post house staff' were established in every district throughout Ulster. They were tasked with signalling and dispatch riding. By February, U.V.F. headquarters were also intent on establishing a group of men in each regimental area, who could travel swiftly in an emergency to other parts of Ulster. Later in the year, the logistics of this proposal would meet with criticism amongst the Mid-Antrim leadership.

Instructions also arrived about preparation by individual volunteers for future 'mobilisations' of the North Antrim Regiment. The letter from Belfast H.Q. advised battalion commanders that a volunteer should:

> 'keep always in his possession some food, such as tinned meat, sardines, chocolate, which in addition to bread or biscuits should serve as a ration for two days if required...'

The letter-writer promised further instructions about 'the best means' of continuing with 'feeding and billeting the men, should they be detained at the place of mobilisation.' Further communication from Belfast H.Q. pointed out the need for a register of men at the drill centre used by each company or at an appropriate local 'alarm post'. The letter also stressed the importance of alerting volunteers swiftly during a mobilisation. Each battalion had to work out its own system for alerting the men, by sending out messengers in motorcars, on motorcycles or bicycles or else on horseback or by foot. Some men were already tasked with gathering

---

163. Correspondence dated 7 February 1914 (Mid-Antrim Museum, U.V.F. archive, MSMAB2011.33.2.24) and (P.R.O.N.I., Arthur O'Neill papers, D. 1239/ 3, 9H, 9L, 215).

'cooking utensils' and 'entrenching tools' to be taken quickly to the 'place of mobilisation.' For the purpose of transporting this hardware, special carts had been set aside. As for the 'entrenching tools', a set of picks and shovels, gathered from local farms and builders' yards, were deemed quite adequate.

Other men were given the job of sending news of the progress of mobilisation to regimental headquarters and thus ultimately to H.Q. in Belfast. To speed up communication, headquarters staff instructed that eight men in each company be trained in semaphore. Telegraphers were to be versed in Playfair cipher code to maximise secrecy. Several copies of maps of the north of Ireland would have to be on hand. These maps would need to be of similar calibration. Orders from now on would refer to the 'Ordnance Survey Ireland Map, scale 4 miles to an inch.'[164]

By now, many men were working flat out to raise the standards of local units, spurred on by the directives from Belfast and by knowledge that the date for the implementation of Home Rule was drawing closer. Robert Orr was combining his job as a drill instructor with the job of adjutant to the entire 1st North Antrim Battalion, in which role he assisted George Young with administrative duties and ensured that company commanders were doing their duty.[165]

One important notice concerned the closure of U.V.F. enrolment in Ulster on 28th February. This closure was to enable leaders to plan their strategy around a stable and well-trained membership. Another notice urged local leaders to ensure that U.V.F. badges were in the possession of all the men, both the 'effectives' and those 'non-effectives' who were contributing necessary support. An accurate assessment of the 'financial requirements' of each battalion was requested by U.V.F. headquarters and this had to be submitted as soon as possible. The workload for George Young, Robert Orr and their colleagues was huge.

By March 1914, the mounted detachment of the 1st Battalion of the North Antrim Regiment was reformed after a winter 'lay-off'. The members of this unit planned to meet each Wednesday and receive an hour of 'cavalry drill' either from Sir Arthur O'Neill or a Sergeant McIlroy. Up to forty men performed on the football ground in front of Ballymena Castle on the first night.

One order from Belfast HQ involved those traders who, all across the province, were 'selling articles, naming them U.V.F. pattern' and thereby increasing their sales. Particularly problematic were advertisements for boots that had been mendaciously described as 'official Ulster Volunteer footwear.'[166]

The threat of British military suppression of the U.V.F. - March 1914

Then towards the middle of March, news broke that the government was sending extra troops to Belfast, arriving on the 21st of the month. The U.V.F. leadership assumed that the soldiers were coming to ensure that the passage of Home Rule took place peacefully. Possibly they would arrest the unionist leaders. The top U.V.F. leaders then took up residence in *Craigavon*, guarded by a group of elite volunteers. All around Ulster, local officers were ordered to 'be prepared to mobilize at a moment's notice.' The R.I.C. were to be kept at arm's

---

164. Details of better U.V.F. communications and mobilisation found in early months of 1914 (Mid-Antrim Museum, U.V.F. archive, MSMAB2011.34.1.2, MSMAB2011.34.1.29-38, MSMAB2011.34.2.110-111) (P.R.O.N.I., the Arthur O'Neill papers, D. 1238/201).

165. Orr is mentioned in this regard in correspondence dated 24 January 1914 (Mid-Antrim Museum, U.V.F. archive, MSMAB2011.34.1.8).

166. Information on the closure of enrolment, finance, badges and mounted troops and warnings to rogue traders are located in correspondence (Mid-Antrim Museum, U.V.F. archive, MSMAB2011.34.2.22-23 and MSMAB2011.34.1.270-275) (P.R.O.N.I., Arthur O'Neill papers D. 1238/142).

length, distrusted as an arm of the government and an ally of the army, now that the British cabinet seemed to be contemplating a direct move against the U.V.F.[167]

George Young received a letter from Sir William Adair, stressing that the police must not be allowed to interfere with parades and must be kept away from training exercises and camps of instruction. Guards should be placed on the gates of parkland where men were drilling. Mounted patrols should monitor the vicinity. Force should be used if necessary, to send any 'snooping' policemen on their way. As the alarm intensified, George Young received a letter from Belfast H.Q., dated 18th March, stating:

> 'Information has been received that the early arrest of the leaders is probable...please take immediate steps to warn your second-in-command, adjutant or other officer, whom you desire should act for you in that unfortunate event.'

An uneasy calm prevailed and a terse further instruction from Sir William Adair, based on communication from Sir Edward Carson, arrived on George Young's desk. In warning the local volunteers to be on their guard, it gave instructions that should the government decide to go ahead with suppressing the unionist plans for self-government '...mobilisation being ordered, the R.I.C. are to be arrested. This should be done by surprise.'

The writer of this missive went on to indicate that the U.V.F. should not fire unless they themselves were fired upon. But units should strongly resist any attempts to arrest their local leaders or seize any weapons. The resistance being offered ought to be non-violent if possible.[168] Then news came through that a number of British officers stationed at the Curragh Barracks in County Kildare had flatly refused to take part in future military moves against the unionists and so it became unlikely that the troops which had arrived in Ulster on 21st March would be used to dismantle Ulster's embryonic provisional government or to 'take on' the U.V.F. in armed combat. At least for now.

Image 42. Ulster Volunteer William Ross, with his two sisters, both U.V.F. nurses: Ulster Volunteer Force hospitals were planned for various locations throughout Mid-Antrim and training in nursing care was undertaken. (Mid-Antrim Museum collection)

---

167. Information on the potential British suppression of the U.V.F. and subsequent 'Curragh Mutiny' is covered in detail in Stewart, *The Ulster Crisis.*

168. Correspondence relating to the looming March emergency (Mid-Antrim Museum, U.V.F. archive, MSMAB2011.34.2.107-111)..

Medicine, uniforms and plans for war

A system of wartime medical care for local volunteers was now being carefully organised. Two hospitals were established in Ballymena and one at Gledheather in the vicinity of Cullybackey, with 69 beds in total among the three venues. Dressing stations were established in five neighbourhoods - Clough, Hillmount, Galgorm, Connor and Cushendall. Money provided by local businessmen went towards medical supplies, including morphine tablets, gauze wipes, chloroform, scalpels, probes, rubber drainage tubes and iodized catgut. Each company in 1st N.A.R. was meant to have two stretchers, as well as a few men trained in first aid with a female nurse in attendance.[169]

And the battalion was about to take one more step towards simulating a modern national army. Amongst several donations by local businessmen, £150 had been provided by Willy Young for procuring fresh equipment and uniform for the local volunteers. By the end of March this material was ready for distribution to all the 'effective' men. The first consignment consisted of 1,000 puttees, 1,000 belts and 'frogs', 1,000 haversacks and 500 leather bandoliers. Initially this material was kept in storage and only handed out to the men when they were due to parade. The firm of Erskine and Sons in Ann Street in central Belfast was used for the transaction, as an order for 1,300 armlets had already been placed with this business in December. Arrangements were made with Hobson and Sons in London to supply 1st N.A.R. with slouch hats. This manufacturer supplied uniforms to the colonial forces as well as working with a number of foreign governments for the purchase of military clothing. By the end of March, 1,000 items of headgear were on their way from London to Galgorm Castle. They had cost 1s/6d each and the bill had come to the grand total of £75.

The absence of guns was now a crucial issue and it was about to be addressed in April. On 7th February however, Sir William Adair had managed to get hold of 45 Vetterli rifles from an undisclosed source. They were of Italian make and Adair wrote to Robert Orr to tell him that they could be picked up from Ballymena Castle and placed at the disposal of 1st N.A.R. But the majority of his men still had no sustained access to firearms. A few days later, Adair told George Young that 1st N.A.R. needed to improvise with all kinds of substitute 'guns' during drill sessions to get the 'feel' of being armed men. The volunteers might even 'use broomsticks when drilling, especially in extended order.'

Adair was unimpressed by the handful of old British .303 Lee Enfield rifles that had also found their way into the ordnance department of the North Antrim regiment. He discovered that the 'back sights' were loose on many of them and that their bayonets did not fit properly. Concern was also expressed in correspondence between O'Neill and Young about the proximity of the adjacent nationalist region, the Glens of Antrim. O'Neill had noted on 1st March that those Protestant men who enrolled in the U.V.F. at Cushendall and Cushendun were 'reported to be over-awed by the Nationalists and...do not drill.' He went on to suggest that:

> 'on a Provisional Government being established, two strong companies from Ballymena should be moved to Cushendall to patrol the glens.' In that event, billeting and feeding arrangements would need to be established for keeping A and B companies of 1st N.A.R. established in the Cushendall area, while C company was placed in Ballymena in order to 'watch the Ancient Order of Hibernians and the police.'[170]

169. Information on medical preparations (Mid-Antrim U.V.F. archive, MSMAB2011.34.1.54-58) (P.R.O.N.I., Arthur O'Neill papers D. 1238/15, 21, 158).

170. Information on uniform supplies and on the inadequacy of the ordnance, prior to the Larne gun-running (P.R.O.N.I., Arthur O'Neill papers, D. 1238/9A, 9R, 9U, 17, 28, 213). Information on the plans to send the U.V.F. towards the Glens of Antrim is located at D.1238/8.

Relationships between police, unionists and nationalists in the spring of 1914

This strained and potentially dangerous relationship with the R.I.C. would seem to have done damage to an attempt to celebrate the contribution of Detective Inspector Ross, who left Ballymena after six years' service during the last week in March 1914. Ross, like every R.I.C. district inspector, had to make a monthly report in which he stated the name, numerical strength and level of activity of every 'secret society' in the district. This may well have placed him deeply at odds with the Ballymena U.V.F., especially if his view of the Ulster Volunteer project was less than positive. A reception was held for Ross in the Parochial Hall, at which he was to be presented with a 'purse of sovereigns.' At the gathering were a number of local clergymen, including Canon Ross and the Reverend Clarke, as well as the J.P. and journalist, John Wier. However there was no sign of D.I. Ross, nor indeed of any of the Young family, who were invariably present at significant social occasions. The decision was taken to 'send on' a cheque to the departing officer, after a few short speeches were made, praising his character in obligatory manner and covering up the embarrassment.[171]

It should be noted that senior R.I.C. figures were invariably Protestant. Often they were far from ill-disposed to militant unionism. A young Monaghan Catholic called John McKenna had recently moved from Ballymena barracks to become a head constable in the coastal town of Carnlough. In 1914 he found himself coming under pressure to gather 'evidence' that the U.V.F. were drilling extensively in his area, which was an unlikely computation in a town where nationalists were so very predominant. McKenna believed that a number of pro-Union officers who headed the county's police force wanted to 'frighten' the British government by inflating the size of the Ulster Volunteer Force. Despite the relative failure of the U.V.F. to recruit and train in the Carnlough area, McKenna's District Inspector would appear to have sent in a report suggesting that there were over a hundred Ulster Volunteers in the district.[172]

Image 43. An R.I.C. badge. The leadership of the Royal Irish Constabulary was dominantly Protestant but the majority of the men were Catholics. Many of the constables who served in Mid-Antrim were from the west of Ireland and a number were Irish-speakers.
(Item housed at Mid-Antrim Museum, on loan from James McNeill)

Close monitoring of the County Antrim police force and of local nationalists continued throughout 1914. Adair surmised - rightly or wrongly - that there had been only 250 policemen in the County Antrim rural district in 1912 but he requested that further research be undertaken on the current numerical strength of the R.I.C. at their various stations. He was also interested in the strength of the local coastguard, presumably with regard to their capacity to interfere with arms smuggling along the coast.

171. *Ballymena Weekly Telegraph*, 28 March 1914.

172. John McKenna, *A Beleaguered Station*, (Belfast 2009) pp 18-21.

Before long a special map had been drawn up by County Antrim regimental leaders, indicating where the local units of the Ancient Order of Hibernians were to be found. The person who created this map noted 170 A.O.H. members in the Cushendall and Cushendun area, 137 in Glenravel, 30 in the Braid area, 60 in Crebilly and a mere 20 in Ballymena. Another 211 A.O.H. members were believed to exist in the rural area between Ballymena and the River Bann. This made for a grand total of 628 men who in all probability were already organising themselves within the ranks of the recently formed Irish National Volunteers.[173]

Meanwhile throughout the first few months of 1914, church parades continued. On one Sunday towards the end of March, local U.V.F. men marched to Killymurris Presbyterian Church and heard the Reverend M.A. Thompson speak. He warned them that in the event of Home Rule, 'the doors of their Protestant churches' might be 'simultaneously closed.' He referred to the words of St Paul in the Biblical book of 1st Corinthians, in order to emphasise the need for genuine and concerted political action: 'I therefore so run, not as uncertainly; so fight I, not as one that beats the air.'

Then, as the pages of *Ballymena Observer* indicate, the Reverend Thompson quoted that much-cherished Bible text which had sustained a Protestant monarch on the eve of the Battle of the Boyne. He told his hearers 'If God was for them, who could be against them.'[174]

A camp of instruction for the local Ulster Volunteers

On 19th April, fifteen miles north of Ballymena, the demesne at Lissanoure Castle, which was owned by the McCartney family, became the setting for a 'camp of instruction', attended by a number of the officers, section or squad leaders within each company as well as other key personnel in the North Antrim battalions - the squad leaders were men who had been placed in charge of smaller groups within each section. The men of 1st N.A.R. assembled at Ballymena railway station, to the sound of bugles and bagpipes, and then travelled north to Killagan station, after which they marched to Lissanoure. Several wagons, containing provisions and entrenching tools, went by road earlier in the day.

While a sentry stood on guard at the gate of the park, the men engaged for three days in a range of activities including lectures on military matters, drill, shooting practice and trench digging technique. Instructors with an army background provided the necessary expertise, including one man who was currently in the employ of the Royal Irish Rifles regiment at Victoria Barracks in Belfast.

Strict rules applied. Predictably, there was to be no alcohol on the premises and rather less predictably, there was a rule that no-one could bring a pet dog along! Each man brought a pillow slip which was 'filled up' with straw on arrival. Palliasses and blankets were provided by the camp organisers. Forty tin wash basins were in place for the men to wash. In the evening, a number of men enjoyed 'sing-songs' around a piano while others played games of draughts, and a gramophone provided a selection of popular music in the background. Some men played football matches, or visited the 'dry' canteen that had been set up on site. There was a temporary base hospital, complete with first aid instructors, who gave advice on the provision of medical services during an armed conflict.

---

173. The information on A.O.H. numbers is recorded on a map (P.R.O.N.I. O'Neill papers, D. 1238/211) and speculation on R.I.C. numbers is recorded in (P.R.O.N.I. O'Neill papers, D. 1238/9X).

174. *Ballymena Weekly Telegraph*, 28 March 1914.

All company commanders, half-company commanders, section and squad leaders were subject to rigorous democracy during their stay, with everyone designated and treated as mere privates. All the men would seem to have been well fed, due to the ministrations of the Bloomfield Bakery from Connswater, who erected a large marquee, lit by 'lanterns', in which they served up four meals a day including a cooked bacon-and-egg breakfast and a supper of cocoa and buns, last thing at night. On 1st N.A.R.'s departure, men of the second battalion of the North Antrim Regiment arrived for a similar course of instruction. During the stay of the two North Antrim battalions, 'cinematograph operators' and photographers were permitted to create film footage and photographs of the camp in operation, with propaganda purposes in mind.[175] Sadly, none of the cinematic images would appear to have survived.

Five hundred and fifty German guns for Mid-Antrim unionists - April 1914

By this stage, the adventurous journeys of Fred Crawford had led him to Hamburg, where the Jewish arms dealer Benny Spiro had procured rifles, bayonets and rounds of ammunition for his Ulster clients. Having completed their purchase, the men who were in charge of this top-secret mission hired a ship which would land most of the smuggled hardware at the County Antrim port of Larne, with the rest being decanted at the County Down ports of Bangor and Donaghadee. Motorised transport from all over the north of Ireland would arrive into these ports on the night of 24th April, in order to carry away the precious cargo, which has been estimated as approximately 25,000 guns, with matching bayonets and a large supply of bullets.[176]

The commander of the County Antrim Division, Sir William Adair, would be in overall charge of the landing and initial distribution of weapons. The U.V.F. in the vicinity of Larne would be key players in this task. The primary task for 1st N.A.R. was to ensure that enough motor vehicles were available to drive to Larne and pick up their own consignment of guns.

The thought of parting with her car was a wrench for Mary Alice Young, who was fearful of what would happen to the beautiful brand-new Vauxhall, which had been specially 'customised' for her in Belfast.[177] It was almost certainly a 'Prince Henry' model, one of the most luxurious cars of the period. The Reverend O.W. Clarke owned a four-seat 'Model T' Ford with an engine capacity of 20 horsepower and he indicated that he would be more than happy to send the vehicle to Larne, to be loaded up with guns before returning to the rectory of St. Saviour's Church in Connor, when the illegal cargo would soon be hidden away from the prying eyes of the police, before distribution to the local U.V.F., many of whom were clearly members of Clarke's own congregation.

Instructions were sent out to all who donated their vehicles, to provide not just a driver but also an extra man to help with loading and unloading the guns and to assist with potential breakdowns en route. In all, 1,000 rifles had been allocated for the two battalions of the North Antrim regiment. This stash was organised in the shape of 200 bundles of five guns each, within which were bayonets for the guns and 100 rounds of

---

175. Information on preparations for and experiences of the Lissanoure camp is to be found in both *Ballymena Observer* and *Ballymena Weekly Telegraph*, during March and April 1914 - as for example in *Observer* on 24 April 1914 . See also (P.R.O.N.I., Arthur O'Neill papers, D. 1238/6B, 27,44, 58). See also correspondence dated 8 and 9 April 1914 (Mid-Antrim Museum, U.V.F. archive, MSMAB2011.34.1.90-94)

176. For a full story of the entire gun-smuggling operation, see Stewart, *The Ulster Crisis* and Keith Haines, *Fred Crawford - Carson's Gunrunner* (Donaghadee, 2009).

177. Dunlop (ed.), *The Recollections of Mary Alice Young*, p 53.

ammunition per weapon. Each bundle of rifles was known to be 105 lbs in weight. 110 bundles were allocated to 1ˢᵗ N.A.R.

Under cover of darkness, on 24ᵗʰ April, the vital exercise began. Although most junior U.V.F. men had no idea what its purpose was, a mass-mobilisation took place and hundreds of local volunteers stood guard at street corners and road junctions, leaving both police and nationalists with little chance of successfully intercepting the gun-running.[178] Only in the homes of the battalion leadership was the real purpose of the mobilisation known. Mary Alice Young and Myra Casement spent the evening praying for the success of the mission and reciting what Mary Alice would later call 'the more bloodthirsty psalms of David'.[179] Already key leaders of the Ballymena U.V.F. such as 'Commander Orr' had arrived at Ballymena and were helping to plan proceedings at the harbour in Larne.[180]

Image 44. A motor corps badge of the Ulster Volunteers. Several vehicles from Mid-Antrim took part in the Larne gun-running of April 1914, including a lorry belonging to Kane's Foundry. (On loan from Alan Stewart to the John Pattison collection)

Fourteen vehicles set out across the Antrim Hills and descended towards Larne, where the ship called the *Clyde Valley* had docked and where at the opulent residence of *Drumalis*, overlooking the harbour, the swift distribution of the guns was being orchestrated. Fortunately for Mary Alice, her much-prized Vauxhall seems to have been omitted from the nocturnal entourage.

The Reverend Clarke's car was the first local vehicle to join the long queue which waited by the dock with headlights blazing. After a quick rendezvous with the men who were handing out the smuggled weapons,

178. Correspondence between company commanders and George Young, April 1914 (Mid- Antrim Museum, U.V.F archive) and other information (P.R.O.N.I., O'Neill papers, D 1238/72).

179. Dunlop (ed.), *The Recollections of Mary Alice Young*, pp 58-60.

180. See Orr's obituary in the wartime supplement to *Ballymena Observer*, 7 May 1915.

the little 20 hp Ford headed back through the darkness towards Connor, carrying rifles, bayonets and bullets. According to one set of recollections by a woman whose grandfather was acquainted with Clarke, the guns were stowed away in the cellars of the rectory, still clad in the bags in which they had been wrapped in Germany.[181]

The next vehicles to rendezvous at the harbour were the two cars owned by the Wilson family of Raceview. Ten bundles were loaded and then the vehicles turned and headed for home. After that, two cars belonging to the Patrick family collected their load and headed towards Glarryford. Then two cars belonging to the Young family pulled into Larne, one loading up with guns for Galgorm and the other heading for Moorfields, to the east of Ballymena. Another vehicle arrived to take guns to Galgorm and then two more cars lined up, bound for the 'big house' known as *Oranmore*.

Two other cars collected five bundles each to convey to *Drumard* and *Hugomount*, which were homes belonging to the Caruth family. Five more bundles then went by car to Moorfields. The final and biggest feat of transport by 1st N.A.R. on the night of the gun-running was the packaging of 25 bundles into a large lorry belonging to Kane's Foundry in Ballymena. The lorry headed off across the Antrim Hills, also destined for Moorfields, which had been designated as a 'pick-up point' for U.V.F. officers from several sub-units, who were tasked with safe storage of the weapons and their subsequent distribution.[182]

Given the much greater strength of the U.V.F., it would have been well-nigh impossible for the R.I.C. to arrest more than a handful of volunteers or impound more than a few of the thousands of weapons which arrived into County Antrim but although the majority of policemen were Catholics and felt no love for the unionist project, there is some evidence that senior officers in County Antrim with a Protestant affiliation were not only quite willing to tolerate but also to assist the gun-running. Head Constable John McKenna, now based in Larne, would later report that his District Inspector in the town was 'walking about the harbour that night, smoking' and, much more controversially, that the 'County Inspector's motor car was there, actually conveying arms to their destination'![183]

Mid-Antrim prepares for battle - April and May 1914

Throughout the spring of 1914, Ballymena's Protestant churches continued to throw open their doors to the Ulster Volunteer Force. On a Sunday early in April, Reverend Haslett preached in the 1st Presbyterian Church to a large group of men which had been marshalled on the Harryville Recreation Ground before marching to the service. The clergyman spoke about the looming conflict with the mighty British Army and compared it to the battle between 'David the volunteer' and Goliath the Philistine giant. He indicated that both were uneven contests. Yet encouragement might be drawn from the fact that in the Biblical story, the young 'volunteer' soldier slew his powerful foe.

During this period, in response to General Adair's call for more relevant and strategic training, 1st N.A.R. staged a mock-battle in which a couple of companies were given white armlets and told to advance on Ballymena from the south-west as if to capture the town. The rest of the battalion were stationed at Galgorm and in

---

181. Clarke's role is documented in correspondence during April 1914 (Mid-Antrim Museum, U.V.F. archive) (P.R.O.N.I., O'Neill papers, D. 1238/9H). These personal recollections were communicated to the author in an interview with the Stewart family of Randalstown (21 January 2011).

182. Correspondence between George Young and company commanders, April 1914 (Mid-Antrim Museum U.V.F. archive) (P.R.O.N.I. Arthur O'Neill papers, D. 1238/9, 72-74).

183. McKenna, *A Beleaguered Station*, p 21.

the Ballymena demesne, wearing red colours as they defended the town against the 'foe.' How exactly the men simulated martial conduct and who exactly was deemed to have won the engagement is not recorded but at the end of the day, the battalion assembled in a field near Galgorm Castle to hear the verdict on their performance from a couple of 'umpires.'[184]

Now the uniform and equipment of 1st N.A.R. was becoming more sophisticated. Tan-coloured leather bandoliers had been purchased from Harper's of Ann Street in Belfast. Each bandolier was capable of holding 50 rounds of ammunition. Water bottles were purchased at 1s/- each and a set of morse and semaphore signalling flags, retailing at up to 8s/6d per dozen. An outfit for the nursing corps had been designed by now, in blue and white colours with an appropriate armlet and apron. A dark blue soft felt hat was part of this uniform and local nurses were advised that it could be purchased from Dalzell's hatters in Belfast's Royal Avenue. A pair of white cotton gloves could be obtained from any draper and a 'long dark blue serge coat' could be bought from McGee's of Donegall Square West in the city.

A list of local doctors had been drawn up. These were men who might offer their services in the event of conflict. This included Drs Armstrong, Stewart, Currie and Kennedy in Ballymena, a Dr McMaster in Broughshane, Drs Dick and Simpson in Cullybackey, a Dr Love in Ahoghill and a Dr McCoy in Clough.

Image 45. A U.V.F. bayonet and scabbard. Thirty thousand bayonets were shipped in on the Clyde Valley, although matching them with the appropriate make and series of gun proved to be difficult.
(John Pattison collection)

In May, the 1st N.A.R., like every other U.V.F. unit in Ulster, was proud to carry its new weaponry in public, in response to Sir Edward Carson's call for an open display of the *Clyde Valley* guns.[185] However, events were proceeding apace at Westminster. The Home Rule Bill, having endured rejection by the House of Lords, was about to become law, due to the restrictions now in place on the upper house's veto, as a result of the recent Parliament Act.

On 25th May, the Home Rule Bill would officially pass. It would then be 'sent up' to the King to sign, although its actual implementation would not take place for some time. But, due to the immense pressure being exerted by the anti-Home Rule movement in Ulster and by the British Tory party, there was much discussion of an 'amending bill' that might grant a degree of temporary autonomy under Home Rule, for several of the

184. Information on Haslett's sermon is found in *Ballymena Observer*, 10 April 1914, and the plans for and execution of the U.V.F. mock-battle are also described in the same paper throughout April.

185. Information on doctors, uniform and Carson's directive regarding guns is found in correspondence belonging to George Young (Mid-Antrim Museum, U.V.F. archive, MSMAB2011.34.2.140), and a variety of memoranda and letters belonging to Sir Arthur O'Neill (P.R.O.N.I., O'Neill papers, D. 1238/ 17-21, 167, 211-217).

Image 46. Frederick d'Arcy, Bishop of Down, Dromore and Connor, blesses the colours of the 1st Battalion of the North Antrim Regiment, at a U.V.F. service held in May 1914, not long after the Larne gun-running. (Young collection, Mid-Antrim collection)

northern counties. The sense of deep uncertainty continued.

On 6th May, a presentation of official 'colours' to 1st N.A.R. took place in Ballymena Demesne. This was a ceremonial occasion which emulated a long British military tradition in which clergy 'blessed' the decorative flag or standard which belonged to a regiment. The colours were presented on this occasion by Lady O'Neill and then the Presbyterian Moderator and the Bishop of Down jointly performed the consecration ceremony. A thousand 'effective' men, who were dressed smartly in their new 'khaki hats', wore their badges, bandoliers and belts and had their haversacks slung over their left shoulders, as they paraded into the demesne. The senior officers wore plumed hats and the colour party carried fixed bayonets. A corps of local nurses made an appearance, wearing their new uniforms and led by Mrs Haughton of *Hillmount*. Sir George Richardson, the overall commander of the Ulster Volunteers, made a stirring speech and congratulated local loyalists on their full participation in the Larne gun-running.

At a U.V.F. church parade a few days later, the Reverend Simpson based his sermon on the scripture verse, 1 Kings 12 v 16:

> 'Now when Israel saw that the King did not listen to them, the people answered the King, saying: What share have we in David? We have no inheritance in the son of Jesse. To your tents, oh Israel...'

Simpson explained how at this stage in Old Testament history, division and secession threatened Israel, idolatry and false teaching abounded and bad government had replaced the glorious reign of King Solomon. He went on to warn that 'real-hearted Christian patriots 'must be prepared to face up to 'self-willed monarchs or a domineering parliament.' If a country's leaders ignored 'the moral law and the just rights and liberties of men' than 'resistance' to authority was obligatory, so as to 'force it back within the limit of the law.'[186]

However, during May, serious discontent with the U.V.F.'s ever more bold strategies was manifested by the Royal Irish Constabulary and by some employers. Sir William Adair received correspondence from the County Antrim police headquarters in Lisburn, criticising the Ulster Volunteers for assembling large bodies of men 'in localities where the peace seems likely to be disturbed' - in other words, in parts of the county which possessed 'interfaces' between strongly Unionist and Nationalist communities.

A letter from U.V.F. headquarters in Belfast on the twenty-third of the month indicated further trouble. Several employers throughout Ulster were annoyed by the disruption to factory night-shifts caused by men going out on nocturnal manoeuvres. The letter advised that such 'experimental mobilisations' should not be repeated.[187]

The Home Rule Bill passes

Image 47. The U.V.F. stamp was placed on each rifle butt and the guns were registered. The leadership aimed to store weapons at central depots and hand them to volunteers as required for parades or target practice. This led to concern about raids on unionist 'arms dumps' by police, the British Army or nationalists.
(John Pattison collection)

By now there was deep concern that the 'passing' of the Home Rule Bill on 25th May could lead to major shows of nationalist strength. At first an order was sent out from Belfast to regimental and battalion commanders such as O'Neill and Young:

'In view of the possibility of Nationalist rowdyism on the passing of the Home Rule Bill, commanders are authorised to take whatever steps they may deem advisable to maintain the peace, and to prevent disloyal processions, burnings, bonfires or other provocative actions or displays taking place in Unionist territory throughout their command.'

186. Information on the presentation of the colours and Simpson's subsequent sermon is found in *Ballymena Observer*, 1, 15 May 1914.

187. These discontents about Ulster Volunteer activity are recorded in the Mid-Antrim Museum U.V.F. archive 23-26 May 1914 in letters from County Antrim R.I.C. H.Q. and from U.V.F. H.Q. to George Young (Mid-Antrim Museum, U.V.F. archive, MSMAB2011.34.2.72-74).

The order was swiftly rescinded. The U.V.F. leadership would appear to have jumped to a reassessment, sensing that murderous local feuds could develop out of such unofficial and extemporary policing of Catholic 'disloyalty'. George Young's eventual word of advice to his company commanders was that they quietly confer with the district commander of the R.I.C. and offer him support in preserving the peace, rather than peremptorily 'calling out' U.V.F. men to undertake random acts of local policing.[188]

In May there was also a strenuous attempt to dismiss lazy or incompetent volunteers. 100 dismissal notices for 1st N.A.R. were sent out during the month. Those local men who had merely been attracted by the new uniforms and the smuggled guns were not, in Sir William Adair's mind, required in the U.V.F. He also sent a letter to George Young, suggesting that 'every man now enrolled adds to the disproportion between numbers of rifles and numbers of men.' Certainly, between the 1st April and the beginning of May, the number of 'effectives' in the battalion had risen from 981 to 1218, including 46 horsemen and 30 nurses. 1,200 'non-effectives' were also in the ranks by now. This was despite the fact that recruitment was meant to have closed at the end of February! But recruitment still continued, despite Adair's words of warning. By the end of July, another 300 'effectives' would join the 1st North Antrim Battalion.[189]

Also in May came fresh instructions from U.V.F. headquarters in Belfast, regarding the 'bataillons de marche' that were to be established in each regiment. These units must be prepared to move at a moment's notice to strategic points of engagement throughout the province. 1,000 men were required from the North Antrim regiment, including over 500 from 1st N.A.R. This was not well received by Sir Arthur O'Neill or by George Young. How could Young's battalion afford to lose half of its best men, especially given that several hundred A.O.H. members existed in or near Mid-Antrim, some of whom were no doubt training in the ranks of the I.N.V.? Negotiations would seem to have continued on this vexed topic throughout the summer months of 1914.[190]

The growth of the National Volunteers and the lurch towards civil war

There is little evidence of how exactly the local Catholic population reacted to the presence in their region of an unofficial, uniformed Protestant army, which was many times stronger in numbers than the police, which engaged in midnight mobilisations, brandished fixed bayonets, carried German rifles and attended church services where their clergy frequently told them that the Catholic church was their mortal enemy and that the desire for Irish Home Rule was the aspiration of a traitor. However it may be assumed that there was considerable anger and fear.

There is evidence of defiance in the ranks of the newly formed Irish National Volunteers. The organisation had swollen in numbers all across Ireland and become a larger if less formidably militarised body of men than the U.V.F. As has already been noted in this account, by the summer of 1914 some 5,000 members were registered in County Antrim alone. It is not clear which bold individuals then took the decision to invite representatives of County Antrim's Irish Volunteers into the lion's den of Ballymena on the first weekend in

---

188. These discontents about Ulster Volunteer activity are recorded in the Mid-Antrim Museum U.V.F. archive 23-26 May 1914 in letters from County Antrim R.I.C. H.Q. and from U.V.F. H.Q. to George Young (Mid-Antrim Museum, U.V.F. archive, MSMAB2011.34.2.72-74).

189. (Mid-Antrim Museum, U.V.F. archive, MSMAB2011.34.1.70-72). For information on battalion numbers, see (P.R.O.N.I., Arthur O'Neill papers, D.1238/81, 153, 171, 197).

190. Local concerns over recruitment to the mobile units requested by U.V.F. H.Q. are recorded in (Mid-Antrim Museum, U.V.F. archive, MSMAB2011.34.1.32,125,126) and (P.R.O.N.I., Arthur O'Neill papers, D. 1238/181).

August, for a meeting at the Catholic Hall, and whether there were any unpleasant consequences for local nationalists. However the choice of venue speaks volumes about growing self-confidence.

In March, at the annual St Patrick's Day Services in County Antrim, a number of Catholic clergy had added their voices to the chorus calling out for Home Rule. In the parish of Duneane, 15 miles south-west of Ballymena, the Reverend J Nolan had condemned the U.V.F. project. Referring to the recent talk of a temporary partition of Ireland, he said 'we shall never accept a measure that would destroy the union of our country.' And he encouraged his hearers by proclaiming that 'the sure light of freedom is bursting forth over the hills and valleys of Ireland.'[191]

By the spring of 1914, the I.N.V. leadership had started its own brief-lived experiment in journalism and volunteers in Mid-Antrim undoubtedly read this journal, called *Irish Volunteer*, stirred by its sentiments and reacting to its instructions. The journal carried various bulletins about volunteer activity around the country and this included news from localities where men drilled up to three nights a week, under the supervision of instructors with a British Army background. Emulating the behaviour of the U.V.F., these volunteer companies often engaged in route marches, parading to their local Catholic Parochial Hall, preceded by a band. *Irish Volunteer* reported how, during a recent meeting of Irish Nationalist Volunteers at Glenarm, an 'enormous multitude gathered from the Glens of Antrim and from Belfast' to assemble in military formation and hear Eoin MacNeill proclaim that 'no power on earth can or will be allowed to slice up Ireland as one would do a dead bullock.'

The newspaper regularly carried advertisements for bandoliers and rucksacks, flags and regalia. There was advice on how to take care of a rifle and instructions to Irish Volunteer leaders about how to create local battalions, companies and squads on much the same pattern as the U.V.F.. There were advertisements for musical instruments for Irish Volunteer bands, including 'war-pipes', sold by Denis McCullough from his shop in Belfast's Howard Street. There were concise articles on Irish history, which focused on 'British oppression' and the refusal of Irish men and women to yield to it. Articles about the women's republican group known as Cumann na nBan also appeared in the newspaper, as did several items of stirring verse:

> 'Oh God grant the day' our brethren pray
> And hasten its arrival,
> When we can stand on our dear land
> Each carrying a quick-shot rifle,
> When cannons shall again belch forth
> And rifle bullets hiss –
> We want emancipation or
> We'll give you some of this...'

A later issue of the paper would echo this strident poetic sentiment, stating that 'The Rifle is the keystone of Liberty.'[192] At an Irish National Volunteer meeting in May, far to the south of Mid-Antrim in the port of Newry, this note had been emphasised by a speaker who had called out 'One man, one gun!'

---

191. *Irish News*, 18 March 1914.

192. Selections have been taken from *Irish Volunteer* weekly newspaper, April-September 1914. See in particular, 11, 18 July, 1 August, 26 September 1914..

Image 48. A bugle belonging to the Irish Citizens' Army. In 1914 the leadership of the I.C.A. began to pass out of the hands of local man, Captain Jack White, into the hands of James Connolly, who was also a former British soldier. (Item on display in Mid-Antrim Museum - on loan from the National Museum of Ireland)

By May, an Irish Volunteer Corps of 200 men had been formed at Glenravel, little more than eight miles from Ballymena. The Belfast-based newspaper, *Irish News*, reported that at Cushendall, on one particular Sunday towards the end of May, 593 'Glensmen' signed up as members of the I.N.V. Because the hall where they were to meet was too small to hold them all, the would-be volunteers marched through the village to the seashore and heard an address which assured them that they were joining an organisation that had 'the welfare of Ireland at heart' and was truly 'non-sectarian.'[193]

In his earlier computations of the strength of opposition that 1st N.A.R would face, Sir William Adair had assumed that 127 Hibernians would have to be tackled in the Glens and that the grand total of Hibernians in all the areas immediately surrounding Ballymena would come to 628.[194] If the numbers given in *Irish*

---

193. Information on the Newry, Glenravel and Cushendall meetings is located in *Irish News*, 19, 26 May 1914.

194. See the estimates which annotate the regional map (P.R.O.N.I., O'Neill papers, D. 1238/211).

News were correct, by late May 1914 there were probably close to 600 Irish Volunteers in Cushendall and Cushendun alone. This would have presented a military challenge beyond the one envisaged by Adair and Young, when they had suggested sending two companies of Ballymena U.V.F. men to deal with resurgent nationalism in the Glens as noted earlier in this account.

By the end of July and early August, the Irish Volunteers had purchased weapons in Europe and shipped them into the country, in smaller numbers than the U.V.F. and arriving mainly at the port of Howth, near Dublin. It is not hard to see that 600 Irish Volunteers from the Glens, even if poorly armed, would have been at strategic advantage on their 'home turf' and could have moved down at night from the high ground above the narrow highways of the glens, blocking the main roads and entrapping two Ballymena U.V.F. companies between steep hills and the sea, cutting off their supply lines and calling for their surrender.

Such considerations lead to the intriguing speculation that the success or otherwise of the U.V.F. in a local military showdown would possibly have depended on the emergence of high-quality leadership. Naively ordering two companies of the U.V.F. to surge forward into the Glens of Antrim might well have ended in a military fiasco and a human tragedy, strangely reminiscent of a certain well-known incident in the Crimean War, involving the doomed charge of the Light Brigade into 'the valley of death'.

In a few months' time, the failure of the British senior officer class in the Great War would be exposed and although recent work by some military historians has offered a more generous verdict on that class and its military performance, nonetheless it is clear that experience gained in Britain's recent imperial wars constituted poor preparation for the demands of 20th century combat. The presence of such men as Adair in the local leadership of the U.V.F. - he was after all a superannuated member of that British military elite - may well have become a severe handicap in the event of civil conflict, despite Adair's efficient skilful management-role in the Larne gun-running. Would he have been capable of imaginative and improvisatory military thinking, when the County Antrim Division of the Ulster Volunteers faced the grim scenario of daily conflict with its nationalist neighbours?

The emergence of hitherto inexperienced but imaginative and efficient military leaders from another social class than the gentry - as in the case of Michael Collins during the later Irish War of Independence - might well have been necessary if the local U.V.F. was to succeed in an era where the rules of armed engagement were changing with alarming speed. Experiences gained by gentleman-officers in the Punjab or at Omdurman would have been of little value.

On 28th June 1914 in one of the very glens for which Adair, O'Neill and Young had planned a possible invasive strategy, Sir Roger Casement gave the annual address at Shane O'Neill's Cairn on Cushleake Mountain. For several weeks he had been reviewing Irish Volunteer units throughout the north of Ireland. On the day of the ceremony, companies from Waterfoot and Cushendall marched over Cross Slieve by the Layde Road to join with fellow volunteers in Cushendun before climbing up the nearby mountainside to the sound of Irish war-pipes, towards the place where the cairn stood, high above the waters of the Irish Sea. Beside the cairn a flag bearing the 'red hand of O'Neill' fluttered on a flagpole.

Then in the course of July, Casement left for America in search of funds for the nationalist cause, just as the Balkan crisis was spilling over into diplomatic conflict between the Great Powers. When international warfare eventually came in early August, he made his way to Germany, seeking support for an armed Irish uprising, plans for which were already beginning to emerge amongst that minority of Irish Volunteers who belonged to

Image 49. Captain Jack White on parade with the Irish Citizens' Army. The militia was formed in 1913 to protect the rights of striking workers in Dublin. By 1914 it was receiving instruction not just in drill but in revolutionary politics.
(Mid-Antrim Museum collection)

the clandestine Irish Republican Brotherhood.[195]

Casement's revolutionary confidante, Captain Jack White, had given up by now on the Irish Citizens' Army, but he had arrived in Derry to train a brigade of men belonging to the Irish Volunteers during the summer of 1914. He organised a 'camp of instruction' in Donegal for some of his men and ended up ' on a wet nocturnal mountainside', cooking teas for them over turf fires and then trying to get them to go to sleep after a rowdy sing-song around the embers.[196]

But although the antagonism between Ulster unionism and Irish nationalism now dominated political life, with added tension given by the intermittent, tense struggles between worker and employer, suffragette issues still featured in the news. The ongoing project to grant women new freedoms clearly frightened some Ballymena citizens, according to a report that appeared in *Irish News* in early June. The article described how:

> 'a number of young ladies who arrived in Ballymena on business on Friday were subjugated to considerable annoyance on account of their being suspected of being suffragettes. They were followed

195. Information on the event at the cairn on Cushleake mountain is found in *Irish News*, 30 June 1914. For further information on Casement's trajectory towards insurrection during the war years, see Dudgeon, *Roger Casement - the Black Diaries*, pp 424-468.

196. White, *Misfit*, pp 213-215.

through the principal streets by a large and mostly hostile crowd and there was much cheering and booing. The strangers, who were respectably dressed and carried handbags had ultimately to secure lodgings in Albert Place. On their appearance on Saturday the ladies were also subjected to considerable annoyance and were followed by a large crowd, whilst the local police were in attendance. The ladies deny being connected with the suffragette cause and state that they represent a firm for the sale of soaps, perfumes etc. Inquiries which have been made confirm this statement.'

Whether or not this story exaggerates the hostility that the unfortunate women faced we do not know but given that *Irish News* was a nationalist organ, there would have been every reason to portray Ballymena as a town with a volatile street-life, ruled by suspicion of any deviation from its civic norms.

Ballymena unionists face the doomsday scenario - June and July 1914

As the last few weeks of peacetime slipped away, the local papers carried news that indicated the potential volatility of the entire county. One night in Ballycastle on the north coast, some Irish Volunteers who claimed that they were protecting the local Catholic convent, were involved in a confrontation with a U.V.F. man called Hutchinson who they said had been offering them dire provocation. The incident had no further repercussions but out of small conflicts like this, larger conflagrations could so easily develop.[197]

All the while, as Sir William Adair reminded George Young in June, nationalist militancy in County Antrim was growing and needed to be monitored: '...the organisation of the Irish National Volunteers must be very carefully watched by all officers of the U.V.F.'

Later, Adair told Young that 1st N.A.R. must prepare a scheme for 'disarming Nationalists' if 'they try to mobilise' and should 'orders be given to do so.'[198] Monitoring the River Bann to the west of Ballymena became a matter of great importance to the local U.V.F. leaders. A particular place of significance seemed to be New Ferry, three miles from Portglenone, deemed to be a likely crossing point for nationalists seeking to make an incursion from the west into Mid-Antrim. Already instructions had been given for local volunteers to 'keep an eye' on all Bann bridges and to 'catalogue' and 'watch' all boats on the river.

Indeed, Ballymena's unionist leaders were starting to think by now about the worst imaginable outcome, which was a widespread domestic war. This would quite possibly follow the imposition of Home Rule and the establishment of an Ulster government. Despite a desire not to waste their precious and limited stores of ammunition, many men were told to engage in target practice, taking advantage of the long summer evenings. A pressing issue concerned the German guns which the Ballymena U.V.F. had been given. A careful record of the two types of Mausers needed to be made, as they matched two very different types of bayonet and at the moment there was considerable mismatch throughout Mid-Antrim.

The leaders at Belfast H.Q. - once again to O'Neill's disgruntlement - demanded that all the Mausers be apportioned to the men of the 'bataillons de marche' whilst the remaining volunteers in 1st N.A.R. ought to make do with the battalion's older rifles, shotguns and small arms. O'Neill signalled his unhappiness not only with this order but also with the large number of men being requested for instant mobility. He suggested

197. *Ballymena Observer*, 24 July 1914.

198. (Mid-Antrim Museum, U.V.F. archive, MSMAB2011.34.2.54,59,60).

that earmarking 300-400 men in each North Antrim battalion was really a more than adequate response and marked the limits of local generosity.[199]

Some of the plans being issued by H.Q. in Belfast showed real fear for the future. On 10th July 1914, a directive was sent out, indicating that in the event of civil strife, there would be a serious refugee problem and that priority should be given to the care of wives and children of 'active UVF men' and those living in 'outlying and exposed areas.' The memo suggested that if refugees could not be safely looked after in Ireland they should be sent across the Irish Sea, possibly before the outbreak of hostilities. Another memo to the County Antrim leaders had indicated that:

'Mr W.H. Lyons of Strandtown...has consented to act as agent for the sending over of any women and children of County Antrim as may wish to leave the country should hostilities occur.'[200]

Whether anyone from the county availed of this facility is not recorded.

Deep fears also existed about the Irish Volunteers' ability to steal U.V.F. guns. A memo arrived on George Young's desk in the early days of July, reminding him to tell his company commanders and their staff not to leave arms dumps unguarded during the Orange festivities on Monday 13th July. Other fears concerned disruption to normal trading patterns in food and fuel, patterns already disturbed during the present crisis. Local merchants had begun keeping their stock of provisions very low, due to fear that the U.V.F. might commandeer the material to feed and assist the 'troops'. It was up to men like Young and his adjutant, Robert Orr, to assure Ballymena traders that no such large-scale impounding of material was about to occur. Another fear concerned transport. By mid-June, in his correspondence with George Young, Sir William Adair was considering the possibility of a breakdown in railway services due to nationalist sabotage. He suggested to Young that 'canals...are less easily interfered with...' and might be quite suitable for the transport of men and freight.

A set of codes for urgent messages had also been established by June, the receipt of which from the 'County Director' would mean instant mobilisation of the Ballymena volunteers. Adair insisted that hospital services must also prepare to go into immediate action. Already a series of Red Cross flags - three feet in width - had been purchased for use at all U.V.F. medical depots across Mid-Antrim.[201]

The actualisation of a unionist 'provisional government' was very much dependant on the ability of areas such as Mid-Antrim to win military contests. These contests might involve conflict with local nationalists or possibly also with the police and the British Army. But there was also the daunting matter of feeding and sustaining the local population until such times as a hypothetical victory had been consolidated. During the summer of 1914, the U.V.F. leadership in Ballymena explained to their superiors in Belfast that there were enough cereal crops in the district, if harvested properly in the late summer and autumn, to feed the population for six months. The grain would be 'ground at watermills in the district' or 'at the steam flour mill in Ballymena.'

199. The priority of keeping a watch on the River Bann and further concern about the battaillons de marche and new worries about ordnance are located in correspondence (Mid-Antrim Museum, U.V.F. archive, MSMAB2011.34.2.21, 24, 30, 32, 51).

200. See correspondence between U.V.F. H.Q. and local command (Mid-Antrim Museum, U.V.F. archive, MSMAB2011.34.2.39-42).

201. Information on fears about the theft of ordnance, the behaviour of merchants, the use of codes and red cross flags, and speculations about transport policy (Mid-Antrim Museum, U.V.F. archive, MSMAB2011.33.2. 43, 49, 50-56, 58 and MSMAB2011.34.2.22, 30, 59-60).

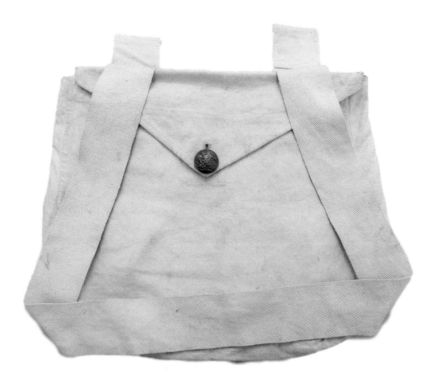

Image 50. An Ulster Volunteer knapsack. Volunteers were meant to carry emergency rations in these bags, especially as the prospect of civil warfare loomed in 1914. Some of the Mid-Antrim battalion were expected to travel out of the district to fight elsewhere in an emergency. (John Pattison collection)

But the long-term supply of fuel for mills and factories would present a problem. Coal from the railway stores and from people's homes might boost fuel reserves in the Ballymena flour mill but it would be gone in weeks, though turf might be some kind of substitute. As the Ballymena U.V.F. leaders pointed out, there was also only two or three weeks' worth of foodstuffs available for local animals, after which the best practice would be to kill and eat them.

But if civil war were to break out at once, before the harvest was ready, the local U.V.F. believed that the absolute 'survival time' for Mid-Antrim might be little more than two months. Then starvation would threaten this part of Ulster unless considerable help was to arrive from sympathisers in Britain. Although correspondence between local U.V.F. leaders and the Belfast headquarters did not go any further with this doomsday scenario, it may be assumed that George Young and his advisors in the battalion pondered the various social maladies that would lie ahead such as looting, and the outbreak of infectious diseases such as cholera and typhus which are associated with malnutrition and civic breakdown and which soon carry off the old, the young and the infirm.[202]

In truth, the leadership of the County Antrim U.V.F. regiment - as of every other unit which cared to engage in self-scrutiny and military prognosis - was 'staring down the barrel' at local war on a scale not seen in Ireland since the 1798 Rebellion and at the possibility of pogroms, reprisals, famine and forced migration on a scale

202. Doomsday scenarios regarding supplies of food and fuel are contemplated in correspondence by the local leadership in response to enquiries by U.V.F. headquarters during May-July 1914 (Mid-Antrim Museum, U.V.F. archive, MSMAB2011.33.2.40-58 and MSMAB2011.34.2.22,30,59-60).

already witnessed during the second decade of the 20th century in the Balkans, where by the summer of 1914, tens of thousands of people had already been 'ethnically cleansed', while the Ottoman Empire continued to crumble and rival national groups competed fiercely for territory.

The last few days of peacetime

However, in certain respects, life in Mid-Antrim went on as before. Enjoying the summer weather, E company of the local U.V.F. held an athletic sports event at The Loopagh, near Cullybackey. The day's activities included putting and 'cricket ball throwing' and they were rounded off by an impressive display of marching. Then, during the usual 12th July celebrations, 1st N.A.R. paraded through Ballymena in front of a Unionist M.P., Walter Long. According to the local newspapers, the men held 'one thousand rifles with bayonets glistening in the sun' as they marched behind a band that played *The British Grenadiers*. Walter Long pronounced that these 'volunteer soldiers' were 'probably the best the world has ever seen.' The round number of 'one thousand' was clearly a rhetorical flourish but it was not too far off the mark. By July 1914, 571 Mausers from the *Clyde Valley* were in the possession of 1st N.A.R. as well as 170 carbines, making for 741 guns in all.[203]

Meanwhile, the refinement of the U.V.F.'s uniform and regalia continued to matter a great deal to the local 'top brass'. The leadership discussed these sartorial issues in July, explaining that as a divisional commander, Adair's armlet was not red but 'blue with yellow markings' whereas Young's armlet, as a battalion commander was 'red with yellow markings.'[204] And still many of the Protestant churches of Mid-Antrim offered their loyal support to the pro-Union cause. On one Sunday evening in late June, the Reverend William Corkey from Belfast addressed a sanctuary packed to the brim with U.V.F. men during a religious service at Cunningham Memorial Church in Cullybackey. His text was taken from the second chapter of the book of Daniel, 'The people that do know their God shall be strong and do exploits.'

The Reverend Corkey assured the men that they were 'fighting again the battle of the Reformation'. During the service, a collection was taken up on behalf of 'the local equipment fund.'[205]

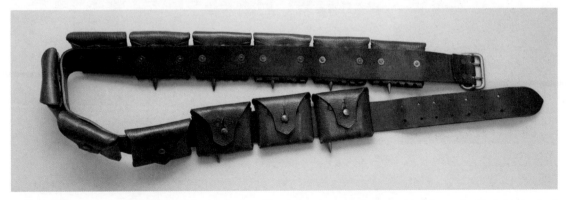

Image 51. A U.V.F. bandolier, for carrying bullets. The limited stock of ammunition from the Clyde Valley had to be conserved rather than being 'wasted' on target practice. (John Pattison collection)

---

203. For public events during June and July, in and around Ballymena, see *Ballymena Observer* and *Ballymena Weekly Telegraph* during these two months. The estimates of numbers of guns in the possession of 1st N.A.R. are found in (P.R.O.N.I., O'Neill papers, D. 1238/180).

204. (Mid-Antrim Museum, U.V.F. archive, MSMAB2011.34.1.11).

205. *Ballymena Observer*, 26 June 1914.

One other congregation showed appreciation of their clergyman during that fateful last summer of peacetime. On 22nd July, Reverend O.W. Clarke, the rector of Connor Church of Ireland, was presented with an appropriately martial gift from the U.V.F. company of which he was the commander. The rectory was decorated with red, white and blue bunting for the occasion and a poem was read out to the assembled gathering before a lady from the congregation buckled a handsome sword onto the waist of their clergyman and their military commander:

'We ask for peace to hold our farms
Our factories and mills
Afar from strife of tongues or men
Among our northern hills.

But if for war our foes are keen
Then let us never falter,
But sacrifice our means and men
Upon our country's altar.'[206]

Image 52. Craigywarren Ulster Volunteers in the summer of 1914, equipped with weapons and fully dressed in U.V.F. kit. The esprit de corps and comradeship are very much apparent. (Mid-Antrim Museum collection)

Many of Clarke's young U.V.F. men would soon have an opportunity to sacrifice themselves for their country. On 28th June, the assassination of the Austrian Archduke Ferdinand had taken place in Sarajevo. The assassin had been a member of the Serb revolutionary group known as The Black Hand, which had been founded in 1912, aspiring to liberate those Serbs who were 'locked' within the Austro-Hungarian province of Bosnia. Their motto was 'Unity or Death.'

---

206. Information on Reverend Clarke's presentation service is found in *Ballymena Observer*, 24 July 1914.

By the first few days of August, Britain would be at war with Austria and Germany, in support of the Serbs, Russians and French. The sacrifice described in that Connor rectory would not happen in the fields of County Antrim but on the beaches of Gallipoli, in the shell-holes of Ypres and in the blood-soaked trenches of the Somme, as thousands of young loyalists from the north of Ireland joined Lord Kitchener's new volunteer army to defend the Empire and to affirm the British identity that they held so dear. They would be joined by thousands of nationalists, who had been advised by their leader John Redmond that support for a war against German tyranny was appropriate for an Irish patriot, and also by many more young men who possessed no political motives for soldiering.

However, readiness to engage in sacrifice would not be the exclusive property of men who put on British Army uniforms in 1914. During the first week in August, *Irish Volunteer* published a poem by a young man named Terence MacSwiney. It was called *Ode to a Bullet*, and in its somewhat convoluted verses, the writer embraced the prospect of dying to free Ireland from Britain with an intense and willing enthusiasm:

> 'Peace we disclaim, that is not conqueror's peace.
> Give us the hurtling war and your sure fate
> Rather than the slave-state.
> Speed on your wings of fire with swift release –
> Yea, with your kiss of pain
> Seek out a secret corner of my brain...
>
> Herald of death, let all war's fury start.
> Let us be free and proud
> Or roll me in my shroud
> Flash in a breath of flame,
> While the white lightnings through the heavens dart
> And find your home in one unconquered heart.'[207]

It was not through exposure to British bullets that this young poet would perish. He would die on hunger-strike as a Republican prisoner in a British gaol, when the Irish civil conflict broke out into open war, after the cessation of European hostilities in 1918.

So as this account of politics, religion and conflict has revealed, when Britain entered the Great War at the close of an August Bank Holiday in 1914, the north of Ireland was on the brink of its own social abyss, in which unionist and nationalist militants increasingly mirrored each other. At a recent A.O.H. meeting at Hilltown in rural County Down, there had been a call for 'the National Volunteers of Ireland to support the long-persecuted nationalists of the North in any action they may deem it necessary to take for protecting their rights.' This was a resounding echo of the words of the Ulster Covenant, in which the right of unionists to use 'all mean which may be found necessary' had been stated.

When, on 29th June 1914, the North Antrim National Volunteers met at Armoy, 23 miles north of Ballymena, their numbers in the far north of the county had grown to 1,000 strong and included 43 horsemen and 38 cyclists. Twenty ladies of the National Volunteer Ambulance corps who were unable to attend received a mention during speeches from the platform. Speakers at the rally emphasised the need for 'defence' rather

207. The poem is found in *Irish Volunteer*, 1 August 1914.

than 'defiance' but suggested that nationalists should 'take no insult' from unionists. The chief speaker at Armoy was that veteran of ideological combat in the letter columns of the Ballymena newspapers, Joseph O'Kane, J.P.[208]

When the representatives of County Antrim's 5,000 Irish National Volunteers met in Ballymena Catholic Hall on the last Saturday of peacetime, they passed a resolution declaring that Irish Home Rule was the 'noblest human cause that ever claimed the devotion, enthusiasm and practical support of Irishmen.' Another resolution condemned the Irish 'ascendency and its dupes.' A collection was taken up for the nationalist 'Arms and Equipment Fund'. Catholic priests were numbered amongst the regional National Volunteer representatives in Ballymena on that day and they included the treasurer of the County Antrim Committee, the Reverend J. Nolan, P.P. who had recently declared at a gathering in Duneane that the Ulster Volunteer program was nothing less than a 'gigantic fraud' and that its rhetoric was full of 'insane threats of violence', designed to make him feel 'an alien' in his 'native land.'[209]

Catholic clergy, like their Protestant counterparts, were now becoming deeply involved in a domestic military project, albeit without any Catholic equivalent to the verbal vehemence that Protestant clerics reserved for attacks on 'Romanism.' The religious and political temperature was nothing less than red-hot.

208. The events at the Armoy and Hilltown meetings are noted in *Irish News*, 30 June 1914.

209. The details of the Ballymena meeting are located in *Irish News*, 3 May 1914. Fr Nolan's speech at Duneane is located in *Irish News*, 18 March 1914.

Conclusion

August 1914 and Beyond

Conclusion
August 1914 and Beyond

Mid-Antrim and the Great War

By 25th August 1914, news of Ballymena's first casualty had been printed in the local papers. The seaman C.G. McConaghy had perished when HMS *Amphion* was mined by the enemy.[210] In Europe, as thousands of highly trained and well equipped Germans thronged into France and Belgium, it became clear that a long war was in prospect. New soldiers were needed from all across the British Empire to assist those troops who had already headed for the continent.

Image 53. A Mauser Rifle, made in Erfurt, Germany in 1892, and belonged to the U.V.F. Shortly after the acquisition of these weapons, scores of Ulster Volunteers from Mid-Antrim would die from wounds inflicted by much more modern versions of the Mauser rifle, when they faced the German Army as British infantrymen in the 36th Ulster Division at the Battle of the Somme. (John Pattison collection)

In September an infantry unit called the 36th Division was formed, primarily to house recruits from the Ulster Volunteer Force. Amongst several poignant church services in Mid-Antrim that autumn, there was a 'farewell' at St Saviour's in Connor for ten volunteers from the U.V.F.'s D company, during which the Reverend Clarke prayed for God's protection for his men in the days that lay ahead.[211] Recruitment levels for the unit varied throughout the district. Urban areas such as Harryville were more fruitful for recruitment than country districts and slow enlistment in rural Mid-Antrim was a source of frustration to Sir William Adair and other senior U.V.F. men who desired to supply more local soldiers for the war with Germany. Eventually, Mid-Antrim as a whole did contribute substantially to the forces but leaving a farm for life in the army was obviously less easy than quitting a job on the shop floor in Braid Water Mill.[212]

For local nationalists who were keen to join the army but very reluctant to enter a division with such an

---

210. *Ballymena Observer*, 25 August 1914.

211. *Ballymena Observer*, 2 October 1914.

212. In the reports on recruitment meetings held in rural Mid-Antrim during the summer of 1915, Sir William Adair and Willy Young often sounded a note of furious disappointment with the local response. See *Ballymena Observer*, 13 August, 27 August and 3 September 1915.

intense unionist ethos, joining a southern regiment such as the Connaught Rangers proved to be a popular option. Amongst the numerous men who eventually left for the front with this regiment were John McAuley from the Clonavon area of the town and Bernard Devlin from Broughshane Street.[213]

By mid-November, news had arrived of deaths at the front among those local soldiers who had been 'called up' in August. It was becoming clear that this European war was altogether different in intensity from the Ulster Home Rule crisis, which for all its sound and fury had resulted in no deaths and a limited number of injuries. Sir Arthur O'Neill was killed in Belgium two months after the commencement of hostilities.[214] On 19th December, Robert Orr went missing while serving with the Somerset Light Infantry.[215] By the early days of 1915, his death had been reported in Ballymena.

As for George Young, he was keen to enlist in the army but had been dissuaded by his aged father from doing so, given the responsibilities of running a busy mill in wartime.[216] In 1915, another well-known loyalist family was devastated as news came through that James Caruth had died at the front, aged just 19.[217] By the end of 1915, scores of local men had perished. The new Waveney Hospital was caring for soldiers who had managed to survive their tour of duty in the trenches but had become victims of the latest sinister weapon of 20th century warfare, poison gas.[218]

In the following year, the 36th Ulster Division took part in the Somme offensive. Their attack on the German lines on 1st July resulted in a ghastly total of over 2,000 deaths and the casualty list included young men from all across Mid-Antrim. As the horror of that long list began to dawn, *Ballymena Observer* lamented that:

> 'No part of the Empire has been called upon to make such sacrifices and endure such trials as is the province at this present time.'

However the newspaper went on to proclaim that:

> 'Ulstermen have proved to the world that they are worthy sons of their forefathers, who fought and won at Derry and on the banks of the Boyne.'

The Reverend W.H. Sloane had the onerous task of speaking at Harryville Presbyterian Church and endeavoured to do justice to the memory of several men who had died in the recent battle. He assured his hearers that on the battlefields of the Somme, these hardy men of Ulster had proved themselves to be outstanding 'northern' warriors:

> 'Who are the hardiest nations on earth? Who are the bravest and strongest? Not those who live in the climates where the sun shines all the time but those in the cold North-lands.'

213. The enlistment of these two men is reported in *Ballymena Observer*, 4 December 1914 and 22 January 1915.

214. www.snakes43.webs.com/weeklywar1914.htm (July 2010).

215. The confirmation of Orr's death was carried in *Ballymena Observer*, 1 January 1915.

216. Correspondence on the issue of whether George Young should or should not enlist, including advice from James Craig (Mid-Antrim Museum, U.V.F. archive, MSMAB2011.34.2).

217. *Ballymena Observer*, 1 October 1915.

218. *Ballymena Observer*, 8 October 1915.

In drawing on the concept of the hardy Ulsterman from the 'cold' north of Ireland, Sloane was drawing on the geopolitical musings of an early proponent of the modern 'Ulster Scots' identity, the Presbyterian cleric, the Reverend J.B. Woodburn of Belfast's Fitzroy Avenue Church.[219]

Sloane spoke to his congregation about one young man who had died called Sam Millar. The minister described him as a true Christian warrior who had organised prayer meetings for his fellow soldiers in the trenches and had sung hymns to lift his spirits when on duty in the front line. He explained that Millar had been: 'fighting in good company, for the greatest hero of the ages was Jesus Christ.'

Image 54. Harryville U.V.F. Roll of honour recording men who joined the U.V.F. and were recruited into Kitchener's new army.
(Mid-Antrim Museum, U.V.F. archive)

---

219. J.B Woodburn, *The Ulster Scot* (London, 1914).

Among those who died on 1st July 1916 was Tommy Haughton from *Hillmount*. A memorial service for Tommy was led by Reverend W.H. Lee, who strove hard to be affirmative throughout, stressing that the boy had been a hero on the 'illustrious 1st July'. Lee stressed that rather than feeling despair, the congregation ought to feel 'joy in the glorious sacrifice.' The Haughton family should also experience, amidst their pain, great 'confidence' that they would one day reclaim their loved one, who had merely 'gone before'.

The Reverend Haslett preached at another of the many memorial services that took place throughout the district in the wake of the Somme tragedy. He spoke of the death of William Grant, who had been such an enthusiastic church worker before his departure and subsequent death with the Ulster Division. Haslett reassured his congregation that Grant now 'sings a happier song in the heavenly choir.'[220]

By the end of the war, Haslett's own 20-year-old son was dead, killed in action in the battle of Cambrai.[221] However other local public figures would have the good fortune to see their sons return unscathed from the conflict, including John Dinsmore, who had one son in the army and another in the navy.[222]

The Easter Rising and its aftermath

During the first two years of the war, activity by both Ulster Volunteers and Irish National Volunteers went into decline. Attention was now focused on news from the front. The U.V.F. still maintained its stock of weapons and observed adjacent nationalist areas with a degree of wariness. By the time that the news of the Somme casualties arrived, Ireland had experienced the 1916 Easter Rising. The decision of John Redmond to offer I.N.V. support for the war-effort had led to a split in the organisation and the growth of a plan, secretly co-ordinated by the Irish Republican Brotherhood, to launch a rebellion which would involve a sizeable number of Irish Volunteers and also Jack White's old comrades in the Irish Citizen Army. They launched an Eastertide insurrection on the streets of Dublin, which was crushed but caused over 500 deaths and much destruction. It was greeted with predictable outrage amongst Ballymena unionists and the local U.V.F. placed a renewed guard on its armouries.[223]

To the distress of his mentors and friends at Galgorm Castle and in the Antrim Glens, Sir Roger Casement was apprehended when landing at Banna Strand on the southern Irish coastline after being decanted from a German submarine. A ship carrying guns for the Irish revolution was also impounded by the British Navy. Tried for treason, Casement was found guilty and executed. His body was thrown naked into a pit at London's Pentonville gaol and covered in quicklime.[224] However by 1916, Casement's old friend in sedition, Jack White, had left Irish politics behind and had been working for some time as a medical orderly with the Australian Army on the Western Front.[225]

220. *Ballymena Observer*'s editorials and coverage of these memorial services for the Somme dead are to be found in editions of the newspaper for 14 and 21 July 1916.

221.   www.snakes43.webs.com/virtualmemorial.htm (3 June 2010).

222.   Interview with the Stewart family, Randalstown (21 February 2011).

223.   Information on the U.V.F. in wartime is located in Bowman, *Carson's Army*, chapter six. For local details, see correspondence of Sir William Adair, referring to guarding the armouries (Mid-Antrim Museum, U.V.F. archive, MSMAB2011.34.4.25-33).

224.   Details on the incarceration, trial and execution of Casement see Dudgeon, *Roger Casement - the Black Diaries*, chapter 16.

225.   White, *Misfit*, p 226-7.

County Antrim stayed relatively calm and unaffected by the Rising. However, as happened elsewhere in Ireland, local nationalists were stirred by this costly attempt to fulfil the idealistic dream of an Irish Republic. They were troubled by the prompt execution of the republican leaders as 'traitors' and angered by the news that Britain was contemplating the introduction of compulsory military service in Ireland in order to fill the gaps in the army's depleted ranks. In due course, a small political party called Sinn Fein, which had supported the Rising, gained support in County Antrim, as it did elsewhere. However, significant loyalty to John Redmond's Irish Parliamentary Party did endure throughout the county during the war years.[226]

Quite a number of women had been active in the Rising and had fired some of the first shots during Easter week. Constance Markiewicz for instance, had grown up as a member of the Protestant gentry in the sort of social setting with which Rose Young would have been familiar. She would go on to become a republican politician and the first woman to be elected to the Westminster parliament. Such levels of militarised female activism on the unionist side were clearly beyond the contemplation of Sir William Adair. On one occasion during the war years, having gathered that a junior U.V.F. officer had been approached by local women who wanted to become more involved in the depleted U.V.F., he told a colleague that 'ladies may prove of great utility at wireless telegraphy etc - but they have no place in the field with troops...' Adair went on to suggest that if this junior officer could 'spare time in which he can afford to teach them flag-waving for their amusement, he can of course do so.'[227]

Meanwhile, utilising the wartime legislation known as the Defence of the Realm Act, the police raided homes and civic buildings in Mid-Antrim. In August 1917, a number of premises in Rasharkin, Crebilly, Newtowncrommelin and Martinstown were visited. Guns and ammunition were seized, belonging to the Irish National Volunteers. The material had been stowed under beds and beneath mattresses but the R.I.C. found the weapons to be of 'obsolete' Belgian make.[228]

By the time that John Redmond died in 1918, Eammon deValera had already become Sinn Fein's first victor at the polls in a by-election brought about by the death of Redmond's brother in a British Army uniform on the Western Front. The modest demands and parliamentary methods of Redmond's party were being eclipsed. To many unionist citizens of Ballymena, Redmond's goals and strategies now seemed benign by comparison with the uncompromising republican politics that was gaining pre-eminence. The local Board of Guardians, made up of representatives from various political persuasions, sent a message of sympathy to the Redmond family. There was general consensus on the board that Redmond had been a 'true son of Ireland' who 'always fought on constitutional lines'. The board members then stood for a minute's silence.[229]

Despite the Rising and the wartime growth of Sinn Fein, reprisals against Catholic or nationalist property would appear to have been rare in the district, with only one case receiving coverage in the local newspapers, which was an 'alleged sacrilege' at Cullybackey chapel in May 1918, when damage was done to the interior of the building and four statues were stolen from the sanctuary then later recovered from a nearby flax-dam.[230]

226. Coverage of an A.O.H. meeting in Carnlough, where Sinn Fein was vigorously denounced, is found in *Ballymena Observer*, 17 August, 1917 and 23 August 1918.

227. (Mid-Antrim Museum, U.V.F. archive, MSMAB2011.34.2.72).

228. *Ballymena Observer*, 17 August, 1917.

229. *Ballymena Observer*, 15 March 1918.

230. *Ballymena Observer*, 3 May 1918.

And still the Great War was going on, with a relentless list of local casualties.

Then in the summer and autumn of 1918, British, French and newly arrived American forces started to make significant territorial gains. At the same time, social unrest and economic meltdown began to destroy Germany from within. On 11th November, an armistice was signed and the global conflict was suddenly over. Victory had been achieved and the streets of Ballymena were flooded with jubilant people. Factory sirens blared. Church bells rang. Drumming parties paraded through the town. Bonfires were lit. Flags were waved in the air and crowds broke into song.

However many townlands, villages and streets in the district had experienced multiple casualties and deep grief. Any attempts to number the Great War dead who have come from a particular region are always difficult but it may be assumed that well over 600 servicemen from Ballymena and its wider hinterland perished in the conflict.[231]

New perspectives

New Perspectives has offered the reader a vista of Irish life under the British Empire, in one particular district of Ulster a century ago. The sections of New Perspectives which deal with local contributions to the unionist project during that era have provided fresh insights into the militarisation of Ulster's pro-empire politics in a location which possessed a particularly challenging diversity of social groups. The local campaign to thwart Home Rule had to unite working-class citizens of Ballymena's industrial labour depots, gentry who occupied country estates such as Galgorm and Shane's Castle, farmers who tilled the fertile fields of The Braid and small-town bourgeoisie throughout the district.

In one sense, this book has portrayed a local political project whose cohesion was made possible by religious and social certitudes that prevailed across much of pre-war Europe and which were about to be destroyed by the Great War and the economic and social turmoil that came in its wake.

In another sense, this book has shown that the subversion of these certitudes was already beginning in the pre-war years. New Perspectives has revealed that new, disruptive developments in labour and gender politics took place in pre-war Ulster and that they were not confined to the urban heartland of Belfast, with its extensive industrial workforce and metropolitan elites. They also made an appearance in a Mid-Antrim community that for all its vaunted modernity, was still provincial and rooted in rural life. The fact that the years from 1911 to 1914 presented examples of working-class people - both Protestants and Catholics - participating in industrial disputes in order to increase their wages and improve their working conditions, laid down a marker for the post-war era. Politicisation of the working man would continue after the war, when in the 1920 local elections, two of the five successful candidates in the dominantly Protestant Harryville district stood on a Labour ticket.[232]

In later years, Labour did not regain that kind of support in a Mid-Antrim where nationalist/unionist polarisation became pervasive, as it did elsewhere in Northern Ireland, and affiliation to an Orange or Green politics trumped affiliation to class-issues. It would be many years before gentrified unionism was supplanted

---

231. Over 600 names of the fallen appear on the comprehensive and illuminating website 'Ballymena and the Great War' which is located at www.snakes43. webs.com (June 2010).

232. Ballymena Observer, 23 January 1920.

by a 'democratic unionism' which explicitly sought to address the bread and butter needs and political fears of the 'ordinary' Protestant man and woman - who in other parts of Britain might well have voted Labour.

New Perspectives, in its acknowledgement of working-class life and the daily struggles over 'bread-and-butter issues', alongside the constitutional tussle of the Home Rule Crisis, has attempted to throw light on the class-based challenges that would always face unionism within its own 'natural' constituency.

This account has also offered fresh evidence of a Mid-Antrim Catholic nationalist tradition that adapted to - but was also prepared to challenge - the amalgam of Protestantism and unionism which prevailed in the district. There has been some evidence in this book that an articulate, educated Catholic citizenship was sometimes prepared to 'take on' the Protestant 'establishment', meeting with stiff resistance, as the 'McCann case' so specifically shows. In due course, with the arrival of widespread tertiary education and professional success amongst northern Catholics in the 1960s, this challenge and its resistance would be renewed with greater intensity in Ulster.

The years from 1911 to 1914 in Mid-Antrim did show evidence of political stances that would not survive, including the values and practice of John Dinsmore, who was rooted within Protestant culture but whose unashamed opposition to the unionist project was tied to a distinctive British Liberal tradition, sharpened by a quasi-socialist verdict that economic exploitation was rife in Ulster and that unionist ideology played a role in protecting class-interest. Such a searching analysis of unionism, coming from within what would later be called 'the Protestant community', was offered from time to time in the years to come. Loyalist ex-prisoners, for instance, during the more recent 'Troubles' were radicalised by incarceration and began advocating a unionism that embraced a consistent left-wing politics.

John Dinsmore lived on until the 1950s, but after the Great War he did not involve himself in local politics and would appear to have put much of his energy into business life and into an issue which was dear to his heart - hospital management. The Ulster Liberal politics that he represented would become an almost forgotten tradition.[233] During the post-war years, the cultural fluidity of people such as Rose Young, whose affection for all things Celtic had flowered inside the Unionist citadel of Galgorm Castle, would also become a rarity. In due course, Rose moved away from Galgorm, living in a house in the Glens with her old friend, Margaret Dobbs, and dying in 1947.[234]

But some embryonic and crucial features of civic and political life in the post-war decades have also been revealed in our study. Many men who had joined the U.V.F. in Mid-Antrim would find a continued role as armed guarantors of the union with Britain, within the ranks of the Ulster Special Constabulary and the Royal Ulster Constabulary. A number of local Irish Volunteers would join the ranks of the Irish Republican Army as it fought against the British presence in Ireland up until 1922. One enduring legacy within unionist culture was that of vivid religious rhetoric, so very obvious on public platforms in Mid-Antrim during the Home Rule Crisis. This rhetoric was more colourful than the language of contemporary 'mainstream' politics, whose discourse was based on parliamentary disputation rather than the vivid declamatory utterances and colourful imagery of the Protestant sermon, in an era when the stirring 'Authorised Version' of the Bible was still widely in use - a text that had been published in the era of the Ulster Plantation and was highly suitable for re-appropriation

---

233. Interview with Stewart family, Randalstown (21 February 2011).

234. Phoenix, *Feis na nGlenn; Gaelic Culture in Antrim Glens*, pp 15, 37.

during the Home Rule Crisis, with its 20th century re-visitation of the tempestuous conflicts of that earlier time.

This vivid religious rhetoric would be a valuable resource for any future 20th century unionist politician who wished to use it, long after such discourse had become ineffectual in the political sphere, elsewhere in the British Isles. In due course, such a politician did emerge within unionist ranks, possessing a sure grasp of Protestantism's pre-war rhetorical heritage and benefiting from familiarity with the colloquial directness of 20th century religious fundamentalism, with its dramatic evangelistic discourse, often influenced by the Southern Baptist traditions of the United States of America, which had become popular in the mission halls and tent-missions of post-partition Ulster. This politician was the Reverend Ian Paisley and he had spent his boyhood in the Ballymena of the 1930s and 40s, where the Home Rule Crisis, as described in this book, was still a vivid, living memory.

By the 1960s, Paisley had entered into conflict with Captain Terence Marne O'Neill, who had become the Prime Minister of the Northern Ireland state in 1963. This son of Sir Arthur O'Neill had been born a few weeks before his father's death. His second forename bore testimony to the Great War in which his father had perished, commemorating the first major military offensive on the Western Front. In the course of his premiership, Terence O'Neill attempted to forge new friendships with politicians in the Irish Republic. He embarked on a series of reforms that he hoped might improve community relations inside northern society and satisfy the aspirations of the Catholic minority. This was met with suspicion on the part of many unionists who felt that Northern Ireland - as constructed four decades previously - was about to unravel and that in this era of reform, their own everyday needs and political insecurities had been left unaddressed by the mill-owners and the squires of Ulster.

In 1969 O'Neill resigned, after near-defeat in an election in the Bannside constituency, in which Ian Paisley, as his opponent, accused the Northern Ireland Premier of a rank betrayal of the Protestant people. Growing up in Ballymena, Paisley had witnessed his father move away from the local Baptist church in order to found his own small, fundamentalist congregation in the town. This breakaway church was situated on the Waveney Road, not far away from the railway tracks and only a short distance from the gates of the Braid Water Mill.[235]

Thus, in the late 1960s, here in Mid-Antrim, where unionist cohesion had been so visible during the period studied within this book, a division in unionist ranks began to open up and a subversion of class-structure began to take place, with long-term consequences for Northern Ireland.

This study of Mid-Antrim has also given ample evidence of the naive and confident trust that made so many young men into Great War cannon-fodder, here and elsewhere throughout the world. Told what to think and how to behave by clergy, gentry, employers, scout-masters, school-teachers, poets and newspaper editors, they volunteered for a war in which implacable imperial rivalry and mechanised destruction were the order of the day and the life of the individual human being counted for nothing. During the Home Rule Crisis in Mid-Antrim, for all its sound and fury, not one drop of blood had been shed. What lay ahead, for all too many young men, was ruthless slaughter.

---

235. Information on the early life and career of Reverend Ian Paisley is located in Ed Moloney and Andy Pollok, *Paisley* (Swords, 1986).

New Perspectives has perhaps provided a very local example of just how unaware humanity really was of the inhumanity that lay ahead in the world's first modern war. However, if the years from 1911 to 1914 were free of bloodshed in Mid-Antrim, the recognition of this fact is not a good reason for ignoring just how close Ulster came to implosion. As a season of Ulster anniversaries and centenaries approaches, it is certainly appropriate for people to remember the convictions, courage and resourcefulness shown by their ancestors and to acknowledge the fact that civic calm and neighbourliness usually prevailed in the most challenging of circumstances. However, mere nostalgia would surely be unsuitable, given the evidence uncovered in this book, of just how close the province of Ulster actually came to the brink of a catastrophic civil war.

Bibliography

Books

Blair, Alex, *County Antrim Characters*, volume 1 (Ballymena, 1993)

Blair, May, *Hiring Fairs and Market Places* (Belfast, 2008)

Blaney, Roger, *Presbyterians and the Irish Language* (Belfast, 1996)

Bowen, Desmond, *Paul Cardinal Cullen and the shaping of modern Irish Catholicism* (Dublin, 1983)

Bowman, Timothy, *Carson's Army* (Manchester, 2007)

Buckland, Patrick, *Irish Unionism, 1885-1923* (London, 1973)

Dudgeon, Geoffrey, *Roger Casement - The Black Diaries* (Belfast, 2002)

Dunlop, Eull (ed.), *John Luke's Harryville* (Ballymena, 1992)

Dunlop, Eull (ed.), *The Recollections of Mary Alice Young (1867-1946)* (Ballymena, 1996)

Elliot, George, *The Tearaway of Clabber Street* (unpublished)

Ervine, St John, *Craigavon: Ulsterman* (London, 1949)

Fraser, P.S.H., *Ballymena 1914-18* (unpublished)

Fraser, P.S.H., *Parish of Kirkinriola; a historical sketch* (1969)

Gray, John, *City in Revolt - Jim Larkin and the Belfast Dock Strike of 1907* (Belfast 1985)

Haines, Keith, *Fred Crawford - Carson's gun-runner* (Donaghadee, 2009)

Lee, J.J., *Ireland 1912-85, Politics and Society* (Cambridge, 1990)

Martin, F.X., *The Irish Volunteers 1913-1915* (Dublin, 1963)

McKenna, John, *A Beleaguered Station*, (Belfast 2009)

Moloney, Ed and Pollock, Andy, *Paisley* (Swords, 1986)

Orr, Philip, *The Road to the Somme* (Belfast, 2008)

Phoenix, Eammon (ed.), *Feis na nGleann; Gaelic Culture in Antrim Glens* (Belfast, 2005)

Scholes, Andrew, *The Church of Ireland and the Third Home Rule Bill* (Dublin, 2010)

Shaw, William, *Cullybackey - the story of an Ulster village* (Edinburgh, 1913)

Sibbett, R.M., *On the Shining Bann*, (Ballymena, 1991)

Stewart, A.T.Q., *The Ulster Crisis*, (London, 1967)

White, Jack, *Misfit* (Dublin, 2005)

Woodburn, J.B., *The Ulster Scot* (London, 1914)

Bibliography

Websites

Ballymena and the Great War (www.snakes43.webs.com/) (July 2010)

Census for Ireland 1911 (www.census.nationalarchives.ie/search/) (September 2010)

Independent Loyal Orange Institution (www.Iloi.org) (November 2010)

Journals

Irish Volunteer

Newspapers

Ballymena Observer

Ballymena Weekly Telegraph

Belfast News Letter

Irish News

Museum, Library and Archive Collections

Mid-Antrim Museum, U.V.F. archive

National Library of Ireland, Casement Papers

Private collection, Rose Young Diaries

P.R.O.N.I., Arthur O'Neill papers

P.R.O.N.I., J.B. Armour papers

Oral Sources

Interview with Brian O'Hara, Ballymena Family History Society (15 February 2011)

Interview with Debroy Barr, Ballymena (12 February 2011)

Interview with the Stewart family of Randalstown (21 January 2011)

Acknowledgements

In the course of researching and writing this book, the author has been indebted to several people, in particular the staff of Mid-Antrim Museum including Debroy Barr, Jayne Clarke, Triona White Hamilton and Shirin Murphy. Members of staff in the Local Studies Department of Ballymena Library were also of assistance as were a number of professional and amateur historians, knowledgeable friends, residents and former residents of the area, all of whom were consulted from time to time. The journalist Des Blackadder helped set the local scene during the period of the Great War, shared his knowledge concerning the involvement of so many local servicemen and their families and was instrumental in helping the museum attain the U.V.F. archive collection. Photographs and portrayals of artefacts from the period have been woven into the narrative, many of which are in the possession of Mid-Antrim Museum. Thanks is due to John Pattison for permitting the use of a number of photographs of his collection of weaponry, uniform, badges and souvenirs from the period and to Christopher Brooke who has provided many key archival material for investigation, namely the Rose Young diaries and the Mary Alice photograph album, both on loan to the Mid-Antrim Museum. To Professor David Fitzpatrick a debt of gratitude is owed for his scrutiny of the text and his helpful comments.

This book has received financial support from the Northern Ireland Community Relations Council, which aims to promote a pluralist society characterised by equity, respect for diversity, and inter-dependence. Views expressed in this book do not necessarily reflect those of the Community Relations Council.

This project has also received financial support from Ballymena Borough Council's Good Relations Unit.